HOT
WOK

HOT WOK

FABULOUS FAST FOOD
WITH A TASTE OF ASIA

Consultant Editor: Linda Doeser

HERMES
HOUSE

This edition produced in 2001 by Hermes House

©Anness Publishing Ltd 2001
Anness Publishing Limited
Hermes House
88-89 Blackfriars Road
London SE1 8HA

A CIP catalogue record for this book is available from the British Library

Publisher: Joanna Lorenz
Project Editor: Linda Doeser
Copy Editor: Harriet Lanzer
Designers: Ian Sandom, Siân Keogh

Front cover: Lisa Tai, Designer; Thomas Odulate, Photographer;
Helen Trent, Stylist; Lucy McKelvie, Home Economist

Photography: Karl Adamson, Edward Allwright, David Armstrong,
Steve Baxter, James Duncan, Michelle Garratt, Amanda Heywood,
Patrick McLeavy, Micheal Micheals and Thomas Odulate
Styling: Madeleine Brehaut, Michelle Garratt, Maria Kelly,
Blake Minton and Kirsty Rawlings
Food for Photography: Carla Capalbo, Kit Chan, Joanne Craig, Nicola Fowler, Carole
Handslip, Jane Hartshorn, Shehzad Husain, Wendy Lee, Lucy McKelvie, Annie Nichols,
Jane Stevenson, Steven Wheeler and Elizabeth Wolf-Cohen
Illustrations: Madeleine David

Previously published as part of a larger compendium, *The Ultimate Chinese & Asian Cookbook*

Printed in Hong Kong/China

© Anness Publishing Limited 1999
Updated © 2000
1 3 5 7 9 10 8 6 4 2

CONTENTS

Introduction 6

Starters & Snacks *14*

Fish & Seafood Dishes *26*

Meat & Poultry Dishes *44*

Vegetables & Vegetarian Dishes *74*

Noodle & Rice Dishes *84*

Index *96*

INTRODUCTION

Most people associate stir-frying with cooking in a wok, and it is certainly ideal for this. However, the wok is far more versatile and can be used for steaming, braising and deep-frying, too. Designed to spread the heat quickly and evenly, it is truly a joy for any cook to use and once you have acquired one, you will probably never want your saucepans and frying pans again!

Wok cookery originated in China, and similar techniques are widespread throughout South-east Asia and India – the karahi or Balti pan being the Indian equivalent of the wok. Many traditional dishes from the cuisines of these countries have inspired the mouth-watering recipes in this book – from Sizzling Chinese Steamed Fish to Khara Masala Balti Chicken, and from Spicy Courgette Fritters with Thai Salsa to Malacca Fried Rice. What they all have in common is a spicy piquancy that will set your taste buds tingling.

The book includes a glossary of fresh and store-cupboard ingredients, some of which may be unfamiliar, followed by a basic introduction to using and looking after a wok, together with some helpful advice on other useful kitchen equipment. Hints and tips throughout the book advise on variations to the recipes and provide guidance on choosing and preparing the ingredients.

You will be both surprised and delighted by the range of fiery, spiced dishes that can be cooked in a wok – but be warned, *Hot Wok* pulls no punches!

INGREDIENTS

Baby sweetcorn Small, young corn cobs have a crisp, crunchy texture and mild, sweet flavour.

Bamboo shoots The mild-flavoured tender shoots of young bamboo are widely available fresh and also sliced or halved in cans.

Basil Several different types of basil are used in Asian cooking. Thai cooks use two varieties – holy and sweet.

Beansprouts The most commonly available shoots are those of the mung bean, but many other beans and seeds can also be sprouted. They add a crisp texture to stir-fries.

Cardamom Available as tiny green pods and large black or white pods containing seeds, cardamom is very aromatic. It is native to India, where it is highly prized.

Cashew nuts Whole cashews feature in many Chinese and South-east Asian stir-fries, particularly with chicken.

Channa dhal This is a round, split, yellow lentil. It is widely available from supermarkets and Asian foodstores.

Chillies The range of fresh and dried chillies is immense. Generally, the larger the chilli, the milder the flavour, but there are exceptions. Green chillies tend to be hotter than red ones, but, again, there are exceptions. For a milder flavour, remove the seeds before using.

Chilli oil This red flavouring oil is very potent, so use it sparingly.

Chilli powder This is a hot, ground spice and should be used with caution. Its fieriness varies from brand to brand.

Chinese five-spice powder The spices are star anise, Szechuan pepper, fennel, cloves and cinnamon. This is available from Chinese foodstores and is different from Indian five-spice powder.

Chinese rice vinegar This is sometimes difficult to find. Cider vinegar is a satisfactory substitute.

Chinese rice wine This can be found in most large supermarkets and Chinese foodstores. It is made from glutinous rice and is also known as yellow wine – Huang Jiu or Chiew – because of its colour. The best variety is reputed to be Shao Hsing or Shaoxing from the South-east of China. Dry sherry may be used as a substitute.

Top shelf, left to right: garlic, ginger, lemon grass, dried shrimp, Thai fish sauce, Szechuan peppercorns, sweet chilli sauce, ground coriander, galangal, Chinese five-spice powder and green chillies.
Middle shelf, left to right: dried red chillies, peanuts, cardamom pods, cashews, peanuts (skinned), kaffir lime leaves, tamarind, hoisin sauce, salted black beans and chilli oil.
Bottom shelf, back row: sake, rice vinegar and Chinese rice wine.
Bottom shelf, middle row: sesame oil, mirin, peanut oil, fresh coriander and cumin seeds.
Bottom shelf, front row: basil, dried shrimp paste, red and green chillies, flaked coconut and creamed coconut, light soy sauce, oyster sauce and coconut.

Coconut milk: An essential ingredient in many Thai and Indonesian dishes, this is made from unsweetened, grated coconut flesh mixed with water. It is also available from supermarkets and Chinese foodstores. It is not the same as the "milk" found inside fresh coconuts.

Coriander Also known as Chinese parsley, a herb it resembles in appearance rather than flavour, it is widely used in Asian cuisine.

Creamed coconut Sold in solid blocks, this gives an intense coconut flavour to dishes. Add a little water to make a thick paste or thin with more water, if required. It is available from most large supermarkets and Chinese foodstores.

Cumin This spice has a strong, slightly bitter flavour. A popular spice used in conjunction with coriander in Indian cuisine, in particular.

Dried shrimp and dried shrimp paste Tiny shrimp are salted and dried and used as a seasoning in many stir-fried dishes. Soak them in warm water until soft, then process in a food processor or blender or pound in a mortar with a pestle. Shrimp paste is a strong-smelling, dark paste with a powerful flavour, so use it sparingly.

Galangal A member of the ginger family and also known as Thai ginger, galangal is widely used in Thai cuisine. It has a less pungent, more aromatic flavour than ginger root.

Garam masala This is a mixture of spices that can be freshly ground and made at home or bought ready-made. There is no set recipe, but it typically includes black cumin seeds, peppercorns, cloves, cinnamon and black cardamom pods.

Garlic This is an essential ingredient in most Asian cookery. Peel the individual cloves and then slice, chop or crush.

Ginger The fresh root is widely available. It has a sharp, distinctive flavour. Choose firm, plump pieces with shiny, unwrinkled skins. Peel the skin using a sharp knife, then slice, chop or grate coarsely or finely according to taste and use.

Gram flour Made from ground chick-peas, this flour has a unique flavour and is worth seeking out from Indian foodstores.

Hoisin sauce A thick, dark brownish red sauce with a sweet, spicy flavour, hoisin sauce is available from Chinese foodstores and most supermarkets.

Kaffir lime leaves Used to impart an aromatic lime flavour to many South-east Asian dishes, fresh leaves are available from Chinese and Asian foodstores. They freeze well. Cut out the centre vein and then cut the leaves crossways into fine strips.

Top shelf, left to right: fresh egg noodles, wonton wrappers, water chestnuts, cellophane noodles, gram flour and spring roll wrappers.
Middle shelf, left to right: dried Chinese mushrooms, pak choi, tofu, dried egg noodles and pancakes.
Bottom shelf, back row: rice, mangetouts, baby sweetcorn, shallots, shiitake mushrooms, Chinese cabbage and rice vermicelli.
Bottom shelf, front row: bamboo shoots, beansprouts, wood ears, spring onions and yard-long beans.

Lemon grass This imparts a mild, sweet-sour citrus flavour. Split and use whole, finely chopped or ground to a paste.

Masoor dhal These split red lentils are actually orange in colour and turn pale yellow when cooked.

Mirin A mild sweet Japanese rice wine.

Mooli Also known as daikon, mooli is a member of the radish family and has a fresh, slightly peppery taste. Unlike other radishes, it is good when cooked, but should be salted and allowed to drain first, as it has a high water content. It is widely used in Chinese cooking and may be carved into an elaborate garnish.

Moong dhal These split yellow lentils are similar to the smaller channa dhal.

Mushrooms Both fresh and dried mushrooms are used in Asian cooking, particularly for adding texture. Soak dried mushrooms in warm water for 20–30 minutes before use. Use the soaking water as stock. Although packets of dried mushrooms seem expensive, only a few are needed per recipe and they can be stored almost indefinitely. Mushrooms are often used more for their texture than flavour.

Mustard seeds These round, black seeds have a very sharp taste and are used for flavouring curries and pickles in Indian cuisine.

Okra Also known as ladies' fingers, bhindi and gumbo, this edible seed pod is a member of the hibiscus family. It is widely used in Indian cuisine.

Oyster sauce Made from oyster extract, this is used in many fish dishes, soups and sauces. It is quite salty.

Pak choi This is an attractive vegetable with a long, smooth, milky white stem and large, dark-green leaves.

Peanuts Widely used in Asian cooking, peanuts add flavour and a crunchy texture. Remove the thin red skins of raw peanuts by immersing them in boiling water for a few minutes. The skins will then slip off easily.

Plum sauce This is a sweet-sour sauce with a unique fruity flavour.

Red bean paste This reddish brown paste is made from puréed red beans and crystallized sugar. It is usually sold in cans or jars.

Saffron Made from the dried stigmas of a type of crocus, saffron is the world's most expensive spice. Fortunately only a small quantity is required per recipe. It has a delicate flavour and aroma and there is no satisfactory substitute.

Sake A strong, powerful fortified rice wine from Japan.

Salted black beans Sold in plastic bags or jars, these salty and pungent beans should be crushed with water or Chinese rice wine before use. They will keep almost indefinitely in a screw-top jar in the refrigerator.

Sesame oil Made from toasted sesame seeds, this is used more for flavouring than for cooking. It is very intensely flavoured, so only a little is required.

Shallots Mild-flavoured members of the onion family, shallots are used in many flavourings and sauces, such as Thai curry paste. Fried in crisp flakes, they can be used as a garnish.

Soy sauce Made from naturally fermented soya beans, this is an important ingredient in Chinese and other Asian cuisines. Light soy sauce is more delicately flavoured and lighter in colour. It is usually used for dipping sauces. Dark soy sauce has a more robust flavour and is used to flavour rich meats and fish. Japanese soy sauce – shoyu – has a slightly sweet, delicate flavour. Malaysian soy sauce – ketjap manis – is syrupy and sweet.

Spring onions These are widely used in stir-fried dishes. The thinner the onion, the milder its flavour will be. Chop off the roots and the top part of the green section, then chop finely or cut into matchstick strips. In some recipes the green and white parts are kept separate for an extra decorative effect.

Spring roll wrappers Paper-thin wrappers made from wheat or rice flour and water, these are available from Chinese foodstores and some supermarkets. Wheat wrappers are usually sold frozen and should be thawed and separated before use. Rice flour wrappers are dry and must be soaked before use.

Szechuan peppercorns Also known as farchiew, these aromatic red peppercorns are best used roasted and ground. They are not so hot as either black or white peppercorns, but do add a unique taste to food.

Tamarind This is the brown sticky pulp of the bean-like seed pod of the tamarind tree. It is used in Thai and Indonesian cooking to add tartness to recipes, rather like Western cooks use vinegar or lemon juice. It is usually sold dried or pulped. The pulp is diluted with water and strained before use. Soak 25g/1oz tamarind pulp in 150ml/¼ pint/⅔ cup warm water for about 10 minutes. Squeeze out as much tamarind juice as possible by pressing all the liquid through a strainer with the back of a spoon.

Thai curry pastes Curry paste is traditionally made by pounding fresh herbs and spices in a mortar with a pestle. There are two types – red and green – made with red and green chillies respectively. Other ingredients vary with individual cooks, but red curry paste typically contains ginger, shallots, garlic, coriander and cumin seeds and lime juice, as well as chillies. Herbs and flavourings in green curry paste usually include spring onions, fresh coriander, kaffir lime leaves, ginger, garlic and lemon grass. Making curry paste is time-consuming but it tastes excellent and keeps well. Ready-made pastes, available in packets and tubs, are satisfactory substitutes.

Thai fish sauce Also known as nam pla, this is used in Thai recipes in much the same way as soy sauce is used in Chinese recipes.

Tofu A soya product, also known as bean curd, tofu is bland in flavour, but readily absorbs the flavours of the food with which it is cooked. Firm blocks of tofu are best suited to stir-frying. Store, covered with water, in the refrigerator.

Turmeric A member of the ginger family, turmeric is a rich, golden coloured root. If you are using the fresh root, wear rubber gloves when peeling it to avoid staining your skin.

Water chestnuts This walnut-size bulb comes from an Asian water plant and looks like a sweet chestnut. They are sold fresh by some Chinese foodstores and are widely available canned.

Yellow bean sauce This thick paste is made from salted, fermented, yellow soy beans, crushed with flour and sugar.

A wok is the perfect utensil for stir-frying because the heat is distributed through the food quickly and evenly. It is also useful for several other cooking techniques, including steaming, deep-frying and braising.

EQUIPMENT

You don't need specialist equipment to produce a Chinese or Asian meal – you can even use a heavy-based frying pan instead of a wok in many instances. However, the items listed below will make your oriental dishes easier and more pleasant to prepare.

Wok There are many different varieties of wok available. All are bowl-shaped with gently sloping sides that allow the heat to spread rapidly and evenly over the surface. One that is about 35cm/14in in diameter is a useful size for most families, allowing adequate room for deep-frying, steaming and braising, as well as stir-frying.

Originally always made from cast iron, woks are now manufactured in a number of different metals. Cast iron remains very popular as it is an excellent conductor of heat and develops a patina over a period of time that makes it virtually non-stick. Carbon steel is also a good choice, but stainless steel tends to scorch. Non-stick woks are available but are not really very efficient because they cannot withstand the high heat required for wok cooking. They are also expensive.

Woks may have an ear-shaped handle or two made from metal or wood, a single long handle or both. Wooden handles are safer.

Seasoning the wok New woks, apart from those with a non-stick lining, must be seasoned. Many need to be scrubbed first with a cream cleanser to remove the manufacturer's protective coating of oil. Once the oil has been removed, place the wok over a low heat and add about 30ml/2 tbsp vegetable oil. Rub the oil over the entire inside surface of the wok with a pad of kitchen paper. Heat the wok slowly for 10–15 minutes, then wipe off the oil with more kitchen paper. The paper will become black. Repeat this process of coating, heating and wiping several times until the paper is clean. Once the wok has been seasoned, it should not be scrubbed again. After use, just wash it in hot water without using any detergent, then wipe it completely dry before storage.

Wok accessories There is a range of accessories available to go with woks, but they are by no means essential.

Lid This is a useful addition, particularly if you want to use the wok for steaming and braising, as well as frying. Usually made of aluminium, it is a close-fitting, dome-shaped cover. Some woks are sold already supplied with matching lids. However, any snug-fitting, dome-shaped saucepan lid is an adequate substitute.

Stand This provides a secure base for the wok when it is used for steaming, braising or deep-frying and is a particularly useful accessory. Stands are always made of metal but vary in form, usually either a simple open-sided frame or a solid metal ring with holes punched around the sides.

Trivet This is essential for steaming to support the plate above the water level. Trivets are made of wood or metal.

Scoop This is a long, often wooden-handled, metal spatula with a wooden end used to toss ingredients during stir-frying. Any good, long-handled spoon can be used instead, although it does not have quite the same action.

Bamboo steamer This fits inside the wok where it should rest safely perched on the sloping sides. Bamboo steamers range in size from small for dumplings and dim sum to those large enough to hold a whole fish.

Bamboo strainer This wide, flat, metal strainer with a long bamboo handle makes lifting foods from steam or hot oil easier. A slotted metal spoon can also be used.

Other equipment Most equipment required for cooking the recipes in this book will be found in any kitchen. However, specialist tools are generally simple and inexpensive, especially if you seek out authentic implements from oriental stores.

A selection of cooking utensils, clockwise from top: bamboo steamer, pestle and mortar, chopping board with cleaver, chef's knife and small paring knife, wok with lid and draining wire, wok scoop

Cleaver No Chinese cook would be without one. This is an all-purpose cutting tool, available in various weights and sizes. It is easy to use and serves many purposes from chopping up bones to precision cutting, such as deveining prawns. It is a superb instrument for slicing vegetables thinly. It must be kept very sharp.

Pestle and mortar Usually made of earthenware or stone, this is extremely useful for grinding small amounts of spices and for pounding ingredients together to make pastes.

Food processor This is a quick and easy alternative to the pestle and mortar for grinding spices and making pastes. It can also be used for chopping and slicing vegetables.

COOKING TECHNIQUES

STIR-FRYING

This quick technique retains the fresh flavour, colour and texture of ingredients, and its success depends upon having all that you require ready prepared before starting to cook.

1 Heat an empty wok over a high heat. This prevents food sticking and will ensure an even heat. Add the oil and swirl it around so that it coats the base and half-way up the sides of the wok. It is important that the oil is hot when the food is added, so that it will start to cook immediately.

2 Add the ingredients in the order specified in the recipe. Aromatics (garlic, ginger, spring onions) are usually added first: do not wait for the oil to get so hot that it is almost smoking or they will burn and become bitter. Toss them in the oil for a few seconds. Next add the main ingredients that require longer cooking, such as dense vegetables or meat. Follow with the faster-cooking items. Toss the ingredients from the centre of the wok to the sides using a wok scoop, long-handled spoon or wooden spatula.

DEEP-FRYING

A wok is ideal for deep-frying as it uses far less oil than a deep-fat fryer. Make sure that it is fully secure on its stand before adding the oil and never leave the wok unattended.

1 Put the wok on a stand and half-fill with oil. Heat until the required temperature registers on a thermometer. Alternatively, test it by dropping in a small piece of food: if bubbles form all over the surface of the food, the oil is ready.

2 Carefully add the food to the oil, using long wooden chopsticks or tongs, and move it around to prevent it sticking. Use a bamboo strainer or slotted spoon to remove the food. Drain on kitchen paper before serving.

STEAMING

Steamed foods are cooked by a gentle moist heat, which must circulate freely in order for the food to cook. Steaming is increasingly popular with health-conscious cooks as it preserves flavour and nutrients. It is perfect for vegetables, meat, poultry and especially fish. The easiest way to steam food in a wok is using a bamboo steamer.

USING A BAMBOO STEAMER

1 Put the wok on a stand. Pour in sufficient boiling water to come about 5cm/2in up the sides and bring back to simmering point. Carefully put the bamboo steamer into the wok so that it rests securely against the sloping sides without touching the surface of the water.

2 Cover the steamer with its matching lid and cook for the time recommended in the recipe. Check the water level from time to time and top up with boiling water if necessary.

USING A WOK AS A STEAMER

Put a trivet in the wok, then place the wok securely on its stand. Pour in sufficient boiling water to come just below the trivet. Carefully place a plate containing the food to be steamed on the trivet. Cover the wok with its lid, bring the water back to the boil, then lower the heat so that it is simmering gently. Steam for the time recommended in the recipe. Check the water level from time to time and top up with boiling water if necessary.

STARTERS &
SNACKS

Quick-fried Prawns with Hot Spices

These spicy prawns are stir-fried in moments to make a wonderful starter. Don't forget that you will need to provide your guests with finger bowls.

INGREDIENTS

Serves 4

450g/1lb large raw prawns
2.5cm/1in fresh root ginger, grated
2 garlic cloves, crushed
5ml/1 tsp hot chilli powder
5ml/1 tsp ground turmeric
10ml/2 tsp black mustard seeds
seeds from 4 green cardamom
    pods, crushed
50g/2oz/4 tbsp ghee or butter
120ml/4fl oz/¹/₂ cup coconut milk
salt and ground black pepper
30–45ml/2–3 tbsp chopped fresh
    coriander, to garnish
naan bread, to serve

1 Peel the prawns carefully, leaving the tails attached.

2 Using a small sharp knife, make a slit along the back of each prawn and remove the dark vein. Rinse under cold running water, drain and pat dry.

3 Put the ginger, garlic, chilli powder, turmeric, mustard seeds and cardamom seeds in a bowl. Add the prawns and toss to coat completely with spice mixture.

4 Heat a wok until hot. Add the ghee or butter and swirl it around until foaming.

5 Add the marinated prawns and stir-fry for 1–1½ minutes until they are just turning pink.

6 Stir in the coconut milk and simmer for 3–4 minutes until the prawns are just cooked through. Season to taste with salt and pepper. Sprinkle over the coriander and serve at once with naan bread.

Seared Scallops with Wonton Crisps

Quick seared scallops with crisp vegetables in a lightly spiced sauce make a delightful starter.

INGREDIENTS

Serves 4

16 medium scallops, halved
oil for deep frying
8 wonton wrappers
45ml/3 tbsp olive oil
1 large carrot, cut into long thin strips
1 large leek, cut into long thin strips
juice of 1 lemon
juice of ½ orange
2 spring onions, finely sliced
30ml/2 tbsp coriander leaves
salt and freshly ground black pepper

For the marinade

5ml/1 tsp Thai red curry paste
5ml/1 tsp grated fresh root ginger
1 garlic clove, finely chopped
15ml/1 tbsp soy sauce
15ml/1 tbsp olive oil

1 Make the marinade by mixing all the ingredients in a bowl. Add the scallops, toss to coat and leave to marinate for about 30 minutes.

2 Heat the oil in a large heavy-based saucepan or deep fryer and deep fry the wonton wrappers in small batches until crisp and golden.

3 When the wrappers are ready, drain them on kitchen paper and set aside until required.

4 Heat half the olive oil in a large frying pan. Add the scallops, with the marinade, and sear over a high heat for about 1 minute or until golden, taking care not to overcook (they should feel firm to the touch but not rubbery). Using a slotted spoon, transfer the scallops to a plate.

5 Add the remaining olive oil to the pan. When hot, add the carrot and leek strips. Toss and turn the vegetables until they start to wilt and soften, but remain crisp. Season to taste with salt and pepper, stir in the lemon and orange juices, and add a little more soy sauce if needed.

6 Return the scallops to the pan, mix lightly with the vegetables and heat for just long enough to warm through. Transfer to a bowl and add the spring onions and coriander. To serve, sandwich a quarter of the mixture between two wonton crisps. Make three more "sandwiches" in the same way and serve at once.

Deep-fried Squid with Spicy Salt and Pepper

This recipe is one of the specialities of the Cantonese school of cuisine. Southern China is famous for its seafood, often flavoured with ginger.

INGREDIENTS

Serves 4

450g/1lb squid
5ml/1 tsp ginger juice, see
   Cook's Tip
15ml/1 tbsp Chinese rice wine or
   dry sherry
about 575ml/1 pint/2½ cups
   boiling water
vegetable oil, for deep frying
spicy salt and pepper
fresh coriander leaves, to garnish

1 Clean the squid by discarding the head and the transparent backbone as well as the ink bag, peel off and discard the thin skin, then wash the squid and dry well on kitchen paper. Open up the squid and, using a sharp knife, score the inside of the flesh in a criss-cross pattern.

2 Cut the squid into pieces, each about the size of a postage stamp. Marinate in a bowl with the ginger juice and rice wine or sherry for 25–30 minutes.

3 Blanch the squid in boiling water for a few seconds – each piece will curl up and the criss-cross pattern will open out to resemble ears of corn. Remove and drain. Dry well.

4 Heat sufficient oil for deep frying in a wok. Deep fry the squid for 15–20 seconds only, remove quickly and drain. Sprinkle with the spicy salt and pepper and serve garnished with fresh coriander leaves.

—— COOK'S TIP ——

To make ginger juice, mix finely chopped or grated fresh root ginger with an equal quantity of cold water and place in a piece of damp muslin. Twist tightly to extract the juice. Alternatively, crush the ginger in a garlic press.

Son-in-law Eggs

This fascinating name comes from a story about a prospective bridegroom who wanted to impress his future mother-in-law and devised a recipe from the only other dish he knew how to make – boiled eggs. The hard-boiled eggs are deep fried and then drenched with a sweet piquant tamarind sauce.

INGREDIENTS

Serves 4–6

75g/3oz palm sugar
75ml/5 tbsp fish sauce
90ml/6 tbsp tamarind juice
oil for frying
6 shallots, finely sliced
6 garlic cloves, finely sliced
6 red chillies, sliced
6 hard-boiled eggs, shelled
lettuce, to serve
sprigs of coriander, to garnish

1 Combine the palm sugar, fish sauce and tamarind juice in a small saucepan. Bring to the boil, stirring until the sugar dissolves, then simmer for about 5 minutes.

2 Taste and add more palm sugar, fish sauce or taramind juice, if necessary. It should be sweet, salty and slightly sour. Transfer the sauce to a bowl and set aside.

3 Heat the oil in a wok or deep-fat fryer. Meanwhile, heat a couple of spoonfuls of the oil in a frying pan and fry the shallots, garlic and chillies until golden brown. Transfer the mixture to a bowl and set aside.

4 Deep-fry the eggs in the hot oil for 3–5 minutes until golden brown. Remove and drain on kitchen paper. Cut the eggs in quarters and arrange on a bed of lettuce. Drizzle with the sauce and scatter over the shallots. Garnish with sprigs of coriander.

Fried Clams with Chilli and Yellow Bean Sauce

Seafood is abundant in Thailand, especially at all of the beach holiday resorts. This delicous dish, which is simple to prepare, is one of the favourites.

INGREDIENTS

Serves 4–6

1kg/2¼lb fresh clams
30ml/2 tbsp vegetable oil
4 garlic cloves, finely chopped
15ml/1 tbsp grated root ginger
4 shallots, finely chopped
30ml/2 tbsp yellow bean sauce
6 red chillies, seeded and chopped
15ml/1 tbsp fish sauce
pinch of granulated sugar
handful of basil leaves, plus extra
  to garnish

1 Wash and scrub the clams. Heat the oil in a wok or large frying pan. Add the garlic and ginger and fry for 30 seconds, add the shallots and fry for a further minute.

2 Add the clams. Using a fish slice or spatula, turn them a few times to coat with the oil. Add the yellow bean sauce and half the red chillies.

3 Continue to cook, stirring often, until all the clams open, about 5–7 minutes. You may need to add a splash of water. Adjust the seasoning with fish sauce and a little sugar.

4 Finally add the basil and transfer to individual bowls or a platter. Garnish with the remaining red chillies and basil leaves.

Spiced Honey Chicken Wings

Be prepared to get very sticky when you eat these stir-fried wings, as the best way to enjoy them is by eating them with your fingers. Provide individual finger bowls for your guests.

INGREDIENTS

Serves 4
1 red chilli, finely chopped
5ml/1 tsp chilli powder
5ml/1 tsp ground ginger
rind of 1 lime, finely grated
12 chicken wings
60ml/4 tbsp sunflower oil
15ml/1 tbsp fresh coriander, chopped
30ml/2 tbsp soy sauce
50ml/3½ tbsp clear honey
lime rind and fresh coriander sprigs,
   to garnish

1 Mix the fresh chilli, chilli powder, ground ginger and lime rind together. Rub the mixture into the chicken skins and leave for at least 2 hours to allow the flavours to penetrate.

2 Heat a wok and add half the oil. When the oil is hot, add half the wings and stir-fry for 10 minutes, turning regularly until crisp and golden. Drain on kitchen paper. Repeat with the remaining oil and chicken wings.

3 Add the coriander to the hot wok and stir-fry for 30 seconds, then return the wings to the wok and stir-fry for 1 minute.

4 Stir in the soy sauce and honey, and stir-fry for 1 minute. Serve the chicken wings hot with the sauce drizzled over them and garnished with lime rind and coriander sprigs.

Hot Spicy Crab Claws

Crab claws are used to delicious effect in this quick stir-fried starter based on an Indonesian dish called *kepiting pedas*.

INGREDIENTS

Serves 4

12 fresh or frozen and thawed cooked
   crab claws
4 shallots, roughly chopped
2–4 fresh red chillies, seeded and
   roughly chopped
3 garlic cloves, roughly chopped
5ml/1 tsp grated fresh root ginger
2.5ml/$^1/_2$ tsp ground coriander
45ml/3 tbsp groundnut oil
60ml/4 tbsp water
10ml/2 tsp sweet soy sauce
   (*kecap manis*)
10–15ml/2–3 tsp lime juice
salt
fresh coriander leaves, to garnish

1 Crack the crab claws with the back of a heavy knife to make eating them easier and set aside. In a mortar, pound the chopped shallots with the pestle until pulpy. Add the chillies, garlic, ginger and ground coriander and pound until the mixture forms a fairly coarse paste.

2 Heat the wok over a medium heat. Add the oil and swirl it around. When it is hot, stir in the chilli paste. Stir-fry for about 30 seconds. Increase the heat to high. Add the crab claws and stir-fry for another 3–4 minutes.

3 Stir in the water, sweet soy sauce, lime juice and salt to taste. Continue to stir-fry for 1–2 minutes. Serve at once, garnished with fresh coriander. The crab claws are eaten with the fingers, so it is helpful to provide finger bowls.

--- COOK'S TIP ---

If whole crab claws are unavailable, look out for frozen ready-prepared crab claws. These are shelled with just the tip of the claw attached to the whole meat. Stir-fry for about 2 minutes until hot through.

Spicy Meat-filled Parcels

In Indonesia the finest gossamer dough is made for *Martabak*. You can achieve equally good results using ready-made filo pastry or spring roll wrappers.

INGREDIENTS

Makes 16

450g/1lb lean minced beef
2 small onions, finely chopped
2 small leeks, very
    finely chopped
2 garlic cloves, crushed
10ml/2 tsp coriander seeds, dry-fried
    and ground
5ml/1 tsp cumin seeds, dry-fried
    and ground
5–10ml/1–2 tsp mild curry powder
2 eggs, beaten
400g/14oz packet filo pastry
45–60ml/3–4 tbsp sunflower oil
salt and freshly ground black pepper
light soy sauce, to serve

1 To make the filling, mix the meat with the onions, leeks, garlic, coriander, cumin, curry powder and seasoning. Turn into a heated wok, without oil, and stir all the time, until the meat has changed colour and looks cooked, about 5 minutes.

2 Allow to cool and then mix in enough beaten egg to bind to a soft consistency. Any leftover egg can be used to seal the edges of the dough; otherwise, use milk.

3 Brush a sheet of filo with oil and lay another sheet on top. Cut the sheets in half. Place a large spoonful of the filling on each double piece of filo. Fold the sides to the middle so that the edges just overlap. Brush these edges with either beaten egg or milk and fold the other two sides to the middle in the same way, so that you now have a square parcel shape. Make sure that the parcel is as flat as possible, to speed cooking. Repeat with the remaining fifteen parcels and place on a floured tray in the fridge.

4 Heat the remaining oil in a shallow pan and cook several parcels at a time, depending on the size of the pan. Cook for 3 minutes on the first side and then turn them over and cook for a further 2 minutes, or until heated through. Cook the remaining parcels in the same way and serve hot, sprinkled with light soy sauce.

5 If preferred, these spicy parcels can be cooked in a hot oven at 200°C/400°F/Gas 6 for 20 minutes. Glaze with more beaten egg before baking for a rich, golden colour.

Spring Rolls with Sweet Chilli Dipping Sauce

Miniature spring rolls make a delicious starter or unusual finger-food for serving at a party.

INGREDIENTS

Makes 20–24

25g/1oz rice vermicelli noodles
groundnut oil, for deep-frying
5ml/1 tsp grated fresh root ginger
2 spring onions, finely shredded
50g/2oz carrot, finely shredded
50g/2oz mangetouts, shredded
25g/1oz young spinach leaves
50g/2oz fresh beansprouts
15ml/1 tbsp chopped fresh mint
15ml/1 tbsp chopped fresh coriander
30ml/2 tbsp fish sauce
20–24 spring roll wrappers, each
   13cm/5in square
1 egg white, lightly beaten

For the dipping sauce

50g/2oz caster sugar
50ml/2fl oz rice vinegar
30ml/2 tbsp water
2 fresh red chillies, seeded and finely
   chopped

1 First make the dipping sauce. Place the sugar, vinegar and water in a small pan. Heat gently, stirring until the sugar dissolves, then boil rapidly until it forms a light syrup. Stir in the chillies and leave to cool.

2 Soak the noodles according to the packet instructions, then rinse and drain well. Using scissors, snip the noodles into short lengths.

3 Heat 15ml/1 tbsp of the oil in a preheated wok and swirl it around. Add the ginger and spring onions and stir-fry for 15 seconds. Add the carrot and mangetouts and stir-fry for 2–3 minutes. Add the spinach, beansprouts, mint, coriander, fish sauce and noodles and stir-fry for a further minute. Set aside to cool.

4 Soften the spring roll wrappers, following the directions on the packet. Take one spring roll wrapper and arrange it so that it faces you in a diamond shape. Place a spoonful of filling just below the centre, then fold up the bottom point over the filling.

5 Fold in each side, then roll up tightly. Brush the end with beaten egg white to seal. Repeat until all the filling has been used up.

6 Half-fill a wok with oil and heat to 180°C/350°F. Deep-fry the spring rolls in batches for 3–4 minutes until golden and crisp. Drain on kitchen paper. Serve hot with the sweet chilli dipping sauce.

COOK'S TIP

You can cook the spring rolls 2–3 hours in advance, then reheat them on a foil-lined baking sheet at 200°C/400°F/Gas 6 for about 10 minutes.

Spicy Spareribs

Fragrant with spices, this authentic Chinese dish makes a great – if slightly messy – starter to an informal meal.

INGREDIENTS

Serves 4
675–900g/1½–2lb meaty pork
  spareribs
5ml/1 tsp Szechuan peppercorns
30ml/2 tbsp coarse sea salt
2.5ml/½ tsp Chinese five-spice powder
25ml/1½ tbsp cornflour
groundnut oil, for deep-frying
coriander sprigs, to garnish

For the marinade
30ml/2 tbsp light soy sauce
5ml/1 tsp caster sugar
15ml/1 tbsp Chinese rice wine or
  dry sherry
ground black pepper

1 Using a sharp, heavy cleaver, chop the spareribs into pieces about 5cm/2in long, or ask your butcher to do this for you. Place them in a shallow dish and set aside.

2 Heat a wok to medium heat. Add the Szechuan peppercorns and salt and dry-fry for about 3 minutes, stirring constantly, until the mixture colours slightly. Remove from the heat and stir in the five-spice powder. Set aside to cool.

3 Grind the cooled spice mixture in a mortar with a pestle to a fine powder.

4 Sprinkle 5ml/1 tsp of the spice powder over the spareribs and rub in well with your hands. Add all the marinade ingredients and toss the ribs to coat thoroughly. Cover and leave in the refrigerator to marinate for about 2 hours, turning occasionally.

5 Pour off any excess marinade from the spareribs. Sprinkle the ribs with the cornflour and mix to coat evenly.

6 Half-fill a wok with oil and heat to 180°C/350°F. Deep-fry the spareribs in batches for 3 minutes until golden. Remove and set aside. When all the batches have been cooked, reheat the oil to 180°C/350°F and deep-fry the ribs for a second time for 1–2 minutes, until crisp and thoroughly cooked. Drain on kitchen paper. Transfer the ribs to a warm serving platter and sprinkle over 5–7.5ml/ 1–1½ tsp of the remaining spice powder. Garnish with coriander sprigs and serve immediately.

COOK'S TIP

Any leftover spice powder can be kept in a screw-top jar for several months. Use to rub on the flesh of duck, chicken or pork before cooking.

FISH & SEAFOOD
DISHES

Sizzling Chinese Steamed Fish

Steamed whole fish is very popular in China, and the wok is used as a steamer. In this recipe the fish is flavoured with garlic, ginger and spring onions cooked in sizzling hot oil.

INGREDIENTS

Serves 4

4 rainbow trout, about 250g/9oz each
1.5ml/¼ tsp salt
2.5ml/½ tsp sugar
2 garlic cloves, finely chopped
15ml/1 tbsp finely diced fresh root
  ginger
5 spring onions, cut into 5cm/2in
  lengths and finely shredded
60ml/4 tbsp groundnut oil
5ml/1 tsp sesame oil
45ml/3 tbsp light soy sauce
thread egg noodles and stir-fried
  vegetables, to serve

1 Make three diagonal slits on both sides of each fish and lay them on a heatproof plate. Place a small rack or trivet in a wok half-filled with water, cover and heat until just simmering.

2 Sprinkle the fish with the salt, sugar, garlic and ginger. Place the plate securely on the rack or trivet and cover. Steam gently for about 10–12 minutes, or until the flesh has turned pale pink and feels quite firm.

3 Turn off the heat, remove the lid and scatter the spring onions over the fish. Replace the lid.

4 Heat the groundnut and sesame oils in a small pan over a high heat until just smoking, then quickly pour a quarter over the spring onions on each of the fish – the shredded onions will sizzle and cook in the hot oil. Sprinkle the soy sauce over the top. Serve the fish and juices immediately with boiled noodles and stir-fried vegetables.

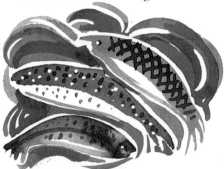

Spiced Salmon Stir-fry

Marinating the salmon allows all the flavours to develop, and the lime juice tenderizes the fish beautifully, so it needs very little stir-frying – be careful not to overcook it.

INGREDIENTS

Serves 4
4 salmon steaks, about 225g/8oz each
4 whole star anise
2 lemon grass stalks, sliced
juice of 3 limes
rind of 3 limes, finely grated
30ml/2 tbsp clear honey
30ml/2 tbsp grapeseed oil
salt and ground black pepper
lime wedges, to garnish

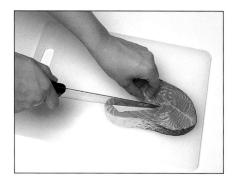

1 Remove the middle bone from each steak, using a very sharp filleting knife, to make two strips from each steak.

2 Remove the skin by inserting the knife at the thin end of each piece of salmon. Sprinkle 5ml/1 tsp salt on the cutting board to prevent the fish slipping while removing the skin. Slice into pieces, cutting diagonally.

3 Roughly crush the star anise in a mortar with a pestle. Place the salmon in a non-metallic dish and add the star anise, lemon grass, lime juice and rind and honey. Season well with salt and pepper. Turn the salmon strips to coat. Cover and leave in the refrigerator to marinate overnight.

4 Carefully drain the salmon from the marinade, pat dry on kitchen paper and reserve the marinade.

5 Heat a wok, then add the oil. When the oil is hot, add the salmon and stir-fry, stirring constantly until cooked. Increase the heat, pour over the marinade and bring to the boil. Garnish with lime wedges and serve.

COOK'S TIP

Star anise contains the same oil as the more familiar Mediterranean spice, anise or aniseed, but looks completely different. Its star-shaped pods are particularly attractive, so it is often used whole in Chinese cooking for its decorative effect. It is also becoming increasingly popular with western cooks for the same reason. It is an essential ingredient in many classic Chinese recipes and is one of the spices that constitute five-spice powder. The flavour of star anise is very strong and liquorice-tasting with rather deeper undertones than its European counterpart.

Thai Fish Stir-fry

This is a substantial dish, best served with crusty bread, for mopping up all the spicy juices.

INGREDIENTS

Serves 4

675g/1¹/₂lb mixed seafood, such as red snapper and cod, filleted and skinned, and raw prawn tails
300ml/¹/₂ pint/1¹/₄ cups coconut milk
15ml/1 tbsp vegetable oil
salt and ground black pepper
crusty bread, to serve

For the sauce

2 large red fresh chillies
1 onion, roughly chopped
5cm/2in fresh root ginger, peeled and sliced
5cm/2in lemon grass stalk, outer leaf discarded, roughly sliced
5cm/2in piece galangal peeled and sliced
6 blanched almonds, chopped
2.5ml/¹/₂ tsp turmeric
2.5ml/¹/₂ tsp salt

1 Cut the filleted fish into large chunks. Peel the prawns, keeping their tails intact.

COOK'S TIP

Galangal, also spelt galingale, is a rhizome from the same family as ginger, with a similar but milder flavour. It is peeled and sliced, chopped or grated in the same way as root ginger. It is an important spice in South-east Asian cooking, particularly in Indonesia, Malaysia and Thailand.

2 To make the sauce, carefully remove the seeds from the chillies and chop the flesh roughly. Put the chillies and the other sauce ingredients in a food processor or blender with 45ml/3 tbsp of the coconut milk. Process until smooth.

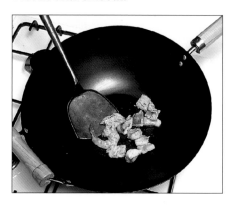

3 Heat a wok, then add the oil. When the oil is hot, stir-fry the seafood for 2–3 minutes, then remove.

4 Add the sauce and the remaining coconut milk to the wok, then return the seafood. Bring to the boil, season well and serve with crusty bread.

Boemboe Bali of Fish

The island of Bali has wonderful fish, surrounded as it is by sparkling blue sea. This simple fish "curry" is packed with many of the characteristic flavours associated with Indonesia.

INGREDIENTS

Serves 4–6

675g/1½lb cod or haddock fillet
1cm/½in cube *terasi*
2 red or white onions
2.5cm/1in fresh root ginger, peeled and sliced
1cm/½in fresh *lengkuas*, peeled and sliced, or 5ml/1 tsp *lengkuas* powder
2 garlic cloves
1–2 fresh red chillies, seeded, or 5–10ml/1–2 tsp chilli powder
90ml/6 tbsp sunflower oil
15ml/1 tbsp dark soy sauce
5ml/1 tsp tamarind pulp, soaked in 30ml/2 tbsp warm water
250ml/8fl oz/1 cup water
celery leaves or chopped fresh chilli, to garnish
boiled rice, to serve

1 Skin the fish, remove any bones and then cut the flesh into bite-size pieces. Pat dry with kitchen paper and set aside.

2 Grind the *terasi*, onions, ginger, *lengkuas*, garlic and fresh chillies, if using, to a paste in a food processor or with a pestle and mortar. Stir in the Chilli Sambal or chilli powder and *lengkuas* powder, if using.

3 Heat 30ml/2 tbsp of the oil and fry the spice mixture, stirring, until it gives off a rich aroma. Add the soy sauce. Strain the tamarind and add the juice and water. Cook for 2–3 minutes.

--- VARIATION ---

Substitute 450g/1lb cooked tiger prawns. Add them 3 minutes before the end.

4 In a separate pan, fry the fish in the remaining oil for 2–3 minutes. Turn once only so that the pieces stay whole. Lift out with a draining spoon and put into the sauce.

5 Cook the fish in the sauce for a further 3 minutes and serve with boiled rice. Garnish the dish with feathery celery leaves or a little chopped fresh chilli, if liked.

Balti Fish Fillets in Spicy Coconut Sauce

Use fresh fish fillets to make this dish if you can, as they have much more flavour than frozen ones. However, if you are using frozen fillets, ensure that they are completely thawed before using.

INGREDIENTS

Serves 4

30ml/2 tbsp corn oil
5ml/1 tsp onion seeds
4 dried red chillies
3 garlic cloves, sliced
1 onion, sliced
2 tomatoes, sliced
30ml/2 tbsp desiccated coconut
5ml/1 tsp salt
5ml/1 tsp ground coriander
4 flatfish fillets, such as plaice, sole or flounder, each about 75g/3oz
150ml/¼ pint/⅔ cup water
15ml/ 1 tbsp lime juice
15ml/1 tbsp chopped fresh coriander
boiled rice, to serve (optional)

1 Heat the oil in a wok. Lower the heat slightly and add the onion seeds, dried red chillies, garlic slices and onion. Cook for 3–4 minutes, stirring once or twice.

2 Add the tomatoes, coconut, salt and coriander and stir thoroughly.

3 Cut each fish fillet into three pieces. Drop the fish pieces into the mixture and turn them over gently until they are well coated.

4 Cook for 5–7 minutes, lowering the heat if necessary. Add the water, lime juice and fresh coriander and cook for a further 3–5 minutes until the water has mostly evaporated. Serve immediately with rice, if liked.

COOK'S TIP

The Balti equivalent of the Chinese wok is the karahi, also known as a Balti pan. They are usually round-bottomed with two carrying handles. Like the wok, the karahi is traditionally made of cast iron in order to withstand the high temperatures and hot oil used in cooking. They are now made in a variety of different metals and are available in a range of sizes, including small ones for individual servings.

Braised Whole Fish in Chilli and Garlic Sauce

This is a classic Szechuan recipe. When it is served in a restaurant, the fish's head and tail are usually discarded before cooking, and used in other dishes. A whole fish may be used, however, and always looks impressive, especially for special occasions and formal dinner parties.

INGREDIENTS

Serves 4–6

1 carp, bream, sea bass, trout, grouper or grey mullet, weighing about 675g/1½lb, gutted
15ml/1 tbsp light soy sauce
15ml/1 tbsp Chinese rice wine or dry sherry
vegetable oil, for deep frying

For the sauce

2 cloves garlic, finely chopped
2–3 spring onions, finely chopped with the white and green parts separated
5ml/1 tsp finely chopped fresh root ginger
30ml/2 tbsp chilli bean sauce
15ml/1 tbsp tomato purée
10ml/2 tsp light brown sugar
15ml/1 tbsp rice vinegar
120ml/4fl oz/½ cup chicken stock
15ml/1 tbsp cornflour paste
few drops of sesame oil

1 Rinse and dry the fish well. Using a sharp knife, score both sides of the fish down to the bone with diagonal cuts about 2.5cm/1in apart. Rub both sides of the fish with the soy sauce and rice wine or sherry. Set aside for 10–15 minutes to marinate.

2 Heat sufficient oil for deep frying in a wok. When it is hot, add the fish and fry for 3–4 minutes on both sides, until golden brown.

3 To make the sauce pour away all but about 15ml/1 tbsp of the oil. Push the fish to one side of the wok and add the garlic, the white part of the spring onions, the ginger, chilli bean sauce, tomato purée, sugar, vinegar and stock. Bring to the boil and braise the fish in the sauce for 4–5 minutes, turning it over once. Add the green of the spring onions. Stir in the cornflour paste to thicken the sauce. Sprinkle over a little sesame oil and serve.

Seafood Balti with Vegetables

The spicy seafood is cooked separately and combined with vegetables at the last minute.

INGREDIENTS

Serves 4

For the seafood

225g/8oz cod, or any other firm, white fish
225g/8 oz peeled, cooked prawns
6 crab sticks, halved lengthways
15ml/1 tbsp lemon juice
5ml/1 tsp ground coriander
5ml/1 tsp chilli powder
5ml/1 tsp salt
5ml/1 tsp ground cumin
60ml/4 tbsp cornflour
150ml/¼ pint/⅔ cup corn oil

For the vegetables

150ml/¼ pint/⅔ cup corn oil
2 onions, chopped
5ml/1 tsp onion seeds
½ cauliflower, cut into florets
115g/4oz French beans, cut into 2.5cm/1in lengths
175g/6oz sweetcorn
5ml/1 tsp shredded fresh root ginger
5ml/1 tsp chilli powder
5ml/1 tsp salt
4 fresh green chillies, sliced
30ml/2 tbsp chopped fresh coriander
lime slices, to garnish (optional)

1 Skin the fish and cut into small cubes. Put it into a mixing bowl with the prawns and crab sticks.

— COOK'S TIP —

Raita makes a delicious accompaniment to this seafood dish. Whisk 300ml/½ pint/ 1¼ cups natural yogurt, then whisk in 120ml/4 fl oz/½ cup water. Stir in 5ml/ 1 tsp salt, 30ml/2 tbsp chopped fresh coriander and 1 finely chopped green chilli. Garnish with slices of cucumber and one or two sprigs of mint.

2 In a separate bowl, mix together the lemon juice, ground coriander, chilli powder, salt and ground cumin. Pour this over the seafood and mix together thoroughly using your hands.

3 Sprinkle on the cornflour and mix again until the seafood is well coated. Set aside in the refrigerator for about 1 hour to allow the flavours to develop fully.

4 To make the vegetable mixture, heat the oil in a preheated wok. Add the onions and the onion seeds and stir-fry until lightly browned.

5 Add the cauliflower, French beans, sweetcorn, ginger, chilli powder, salt, green chillies and fresh coriander. Stir-fry for about 7–10 minutes over a medium heat, making sure that the cauliflower florets retain their shape.

6 Spoon the fried vegetables around the edge of a shallow dish, leaving a space in the middle for the seafood, and keep warm.

7 Wash and dry the pan, then heat the oil to fry the seafood pieces. Fry the seafood pieces in two or three batches, until they turn a golden brown. Remove with a slotted spoon and drain on kitchen paper.

8 Arrange each batch of seafood in the middle of the dish of vegetables and keep warm while you fry the remaining batches. Garnish with lime slices and serve immediately.

Malaysian Fish Curry

Fish gently cooked in a wok of coconut milk makes a mouth-watering curry for any occasion.

INGREDIENTS

Serves 4–6

675g/1¹/₂lb monkfish, hokey or
   red snapper fillet
salt, to taste
45ml/3 tbsp grated or
   desiccated coconut
30ml/2 tbsp vegetable oil
2.5cm/1in galangal or fresh root ginger,
   peeled and thinly sliced
2 small red chillies, seeded and
   finely chopped
2 cloves garlic, crushed
5cm/2in lemon grass stalk, shredded
1 piece shrimp paste, 1cm/¹/₂in square
   or 15ml/1 tbsp fish sauce
400g/14oz canned coconut milk
600ml/1 pint/2¹/₂ cups chicken stock
2.5ml/¹/₂ tsp turmeric
15ml/1 tbsp sugar
juice of 1 lime, or ¹/₂ lemon
boiled rice, to serve (optional)

1 Cut the fish into large chunks, season with salt and set aside.

COOK'S TIP

Sambal, a fiery hot relish, is traditionally served with this curry. Mix together 2 skinned and chopped tomatoes, 1 finely chopped onion, 1 finely chopped green chilli and 30ml/2 tbsp lime juice. Season to taste with salt and pepper and sprinkle over 30ml/2 tbsp grated or desiccated coconut.

2 Dry fry the coconut in a large wok until evenly brown. Add the vegetable oil, galangal or ginger, chillies, garlic and lemon grass and fry briefly. Stir in the shrimp paste or fish sauce. Strain the coconut milk through a sieve, then add to the wok.

3 Add the chicken stock, turmeric, sugar, a little salt and the lime or lemon juice. Simmer for 10 minutes. Add the fish and simmer for 6–8 minutes. Stir in the thick part of the coconut milk and simmer to thicken. Garnish with coriander and lime slices and serve with rice, if liked.

Vinegar Fish

Fish cooked in a spicy mixture that includes chillies, ginger and vinegar is an Indonesian speciality. It is a method that lends itself particularly well to strong-flavoured, oily fish, such as the mackerel used here.

INGREDIENTS

Serves 2–3

2–3 mackerel, filleted
2-3 red chillies, seeded
4 macadamia nuts or 8 almonds
1 red onion, quartered
2 garlic cloves, crushed
1cm/½in piece root ginger, peeled and sliced
5ml/1 tsp ground turmeric
45ml/3 tbsp coconut or vegetable oil
45ml/3 tbsp wine vinegar
150ml/¼ pint/⅔ cup water
salt
deep-fried onions and finely chopped chilli, to garnish
boiled or coconut rice, to serve (optional)

1 Rinse the mackerel fillets in cold water and dry well on kitchen paper. Set aside.

COOK'S TIP

To make coconut rice, put 400g/14oz washed long grain rice in a heavy saucepan with 2.5ml/½ tsp salt, a 5cm/2in piece of lemon grass and 25g/1oz creamed coconut. Add 750ml/1¼ pints/3 cups boiling water and stir once to prevent the grains sticking together. Simmer over a medium heat for 10–12 minutes. Remove the pan from the heat, cover and set aside for 5 minutes. Fluff the rice with a fork or chopsticks before serving.

2 Put the chillies, macadamia nuts or almonds, onion, garlic, ginger, turmeric and 15ml/1 tbsp of the oil in a food processor and process to form a paste. Alternatively, pound them together in a mortar with a pestle to form a paste. Heat the remaining oil in a wok. When it is hot, add the paste and cook for 1–2 minutes without browning. Stir in the vinegar and water and season with salt to taste. Bring to the boil, then lower the heat.

3 Add the mackerel fillets to the sauce and simmer for 6–8 minutes or until the fish is tender and cooked.

4 Transfer the fish to a warm serving dish. Bring the sauce to a boil and cook for 1 minute or until it has reduced slightly. Pour the sauce over the fish, garnish with the deep-fried onions and chopped chilli and serve with rice, if liked.

Balti Prawns in Hot Sauce

This sizzling prawn dish is cooked in a fiery hot and spicy sauce. Not only does the sauce contain chilli powder, it is further enhanced by the addition of ground green chillies and other spices.

INGREDIENTS

Serves 4

2 onions, roughly chopped
30ml/2 tbsp tomato purée
5ml/1 tsp ground coriander
1.5ml/¼ tsp turmeric
5ml/1 tsp chilli powder
3 fresh green chillies
45ml/3 tbsp chopped fresh coriander
30ml/2 tbsp lemon juice
5ml/1 tsp salt
45ml/3 tbsp corn oil
16 peeled cooked king prawns

1 Put the onions, tomato purée, ground coriander, turmeric, chilli powder, 2 of the green chillies, 30ml/2 tbsp of the chopped coriander, the lemon juice and salt into a food processor. Process for about 1 minute. If the mixture seems too thick, add a little water to loosen it. Chop the remaining chilli and reserve for garnishing the dish.

2 Heat the oil in a preheated wok or frying pan. Lower the heat, add the spice mixture and fry for 3–5 minutes or until the sauce has thickened slightly.

3 Add the prawns and stir-fry over a medium heat until they are heated through, but not overcooked.

4 Transfer to a serving dish and garnish with the remaining chilli and chopped fresh coriander. Serve immediately.

Spiced Prawns with Coconut

This spicy dish is based on the traditional Indonesian dish *sambal goreng udang*. Sambals are pungent, very hot dishes popular throughout south India and South-east Asia.

INGREDIENTS

Serves 3–4

2–3 red chillies, seeded and chopped
3 shallots, chopped
1 lemon grass stalk, chopped
2 garlic cloves, chopped
thin sliver of dried shrimp paste
2.5ml/½ tsp ground galangal
5ml/1 tsp ground turmeric
5ml/1 tsp ground coriander
15ml/1 tbsp groundnut oil
250ml/8fl oz/1 cup water
2 fresh kaffir lime leaves
5ml/1 tsp light brown soft sugar
2 tomatoes, skinned, seeded
    and chopped
250ml/8fl oz/1 cup coconut milk
675g/1½lb large raw prawns, peeled
    and deveined
squeeze of lemon juice
salt
shredded spring onions and flaked
    coconut, to garnish

1 In a mortar, pound together the chillies, shallots, lemon grass, garlic, shrimp paste, galangal, turmeric and coriander with a pestle until the mixture forms a paste.

2 Heat a wok, add the oil and swirl it around. Add the spice paste and stir-fry for 2 minutes. Pour in the water and add the kaffir lime leaves, sugar and tomatoes. Simmer for 8–10 minutes until most of the liquid has evaporated.

--- COOK'S TIP ---

Dried shrimp paste, widely used in South-east Asian cooking, is available from oriental food stores. Ground galangal, which is similar to ground ginger and comes from the same family, is also available from oriental food stores.

3 Add the coconut milk and prawns and cook gently, stirring, for 4 minutes until the prawns are pink. Season with lemon juice and salt to taste. Transfer the mixture to a warmed serving dish, garnish with the spring onions and flaked coconut and serve.

Oriental Scallops with Ginger Relish

Buy scallops in their shells to be absolutely sure of their freshness; your fishmonger will open them for you if you find this difficult. Remember to ask for the shells, which make excellent and attractive serving dishes. Queen scallops are particularly prized for their delicate-tasting coral or roe.

INGREDIENTS

Serves 4
8 king or queen scallops
4 whole star anise
25g/1oz unsalted butter
salt and ground white pepper
fresh chervil sprigs and whole star anise, to garnish

For the relish
$^1/_2$ cucumber, peeled
salt, for sprinkling
5cm/2in fresh root ginger, peeled
10ml/2 tsp caster sugar
45ml/3 tbsp rice wine vinegar
10ml/2 tsp ginger juice, strained from a jar of stem ginger
sesame seeds, to garnish

1 To make the relish, halve the cucumber lengthways and scoop out the seeds with a teaspoon and discard.

2 Cut the cucumber into 2.5cm/1in pieces, place in a colander and sprinkle liberally with salt. Set aside for 30 minutes.

3 Open the scallop shells, detach the scallops and remove the edible parts. Cut each scallop into two or three slices and reserve the corals. Coarsely grind the star anise in a mortar with a pestle.

4 Place the scallop slices and corals in a bowl, sprinkle over the star anise and season with salt and pepper. Set aside to marinate for about 1 hour.

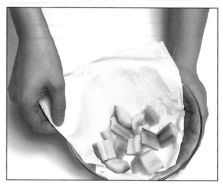

5 Rinse the cucumber under cold water, drain well and pat dry on kitchen paper. Cut the ginger into thin julienne strips and mix with the cucumber, sugar, vinegar and ginger juice. Cover and chill until needed.

6 Heat a wok and add the butter. When the butter is hot, add the scallop slices and corals and stir-fry for 2–3 minutes. Garnish with sprigs of chervil and whole star anise, and serve with the cucumber relish, sprinkled with sesame seeds.

COOK'S TIP

To prepare scallops, hold the shell, flat side up, and insert a strong knife between the shells to cut through the muscle. Separate the two shells. Slide the knife blade underneath the scallop in the bottom shell to cut the second muscle. Remove the scallop and separate the edible parts – the white muscle and orange coral or roe. The skirt can be used for making fish stock, but the other parts should be discarded.

Chilli Crabs

It is possible to find variations on *Kepitang Pedas* all over Asia. It will be memorable whether you eat in simple surroundings or in a sophisticated restaurant.

INGREDIENTS

Serves 4

2 cooked crabs, about 675g/1½lb
1cm/½in cube *terasi*
2 garlic cloves
2 fresh red chillies, seeded, or 5ml/
    1 tsp chopped chilli from a jar
1cm/½in fresh root ginger, peeled
    and sliced
60ml/4 tbsp sunflower oil
300ml/½ pint/1¼ cups tomato ketchup
15ml/1 tbsp dark brown sugar
150ml/¼ pint/⅔ cup warm water
4 spring onions, chopped, to garnish
cucumber chunks and hot toast,
    to serve (optional)

1 Remove the large claws of one crab and turn on to its back, with the head facing away from you. Use your thumbs to push the body up from the main shell. Discard the stomach sac and "dead men's fingers", i.e. lungs and any green matter. Leave the creamy brown meat in the shell and cut the shell in half, with a cleaver or strong knife. Cut the body section in half and crack the claws with a sharp blow from a hammer or cleaver. Avoid splintering the claws. Repeat with the other crab.

2 Grind the *terasi*, garlic, chillies and ginger to a paste in a food processor or with a pestle and mortar.

3 Heat a wok and add the oil. Fry the spice paste, stirring it all the time, without browning.

4 Stir in the tomato ketchup, sugar and water and mix the sauce well. When just boiling, add all the crab pieces and toss in the sauce until well-coated and hot. Serve in a large bowl, sprinkled with the spring onions. Place in the centre of the table for everyone to help themselves. Accompany this finger-licking dish with cool cucumber chunks and hot toast for mopping up the sauce, if you like.

Stir-fried Prawns with Tamarind

The sour, tangy flavour that is characteristic of many Thai dishes comes from tamarind. Fresh tamarind pods from the tamarind tree can sometimes be bought, but preparing them for cooking is a laborious process. The Thais, however, usually prefer to use compressed blocks of tamarind paste, which is simply soaked in warm water and then strained.

INGREDIENTS

Serves 4–6

50g/2oz tamarind paste
150ml/¼ pint/⅔ cup boiling water
30ml/2 tbsp vegetable oil
30ml/2 tbsp chopped onion
30ml/2 tbsp palm sugar
30ml/2 tbsp chicken stock or water
15ml/1 tbsp fish sauce
6 dried red chillies, fried
450g/1lb uncooked shelled prawns
15ml/1 tbsp fried chopped garlic
30ml/2 tbsp fried sliced shallots
2 spring onions, chopped, to garnish

1 Put the tamarind paste in a small bowl, pour over the boiling water and stir well to break up any lumps. Leave for 30 minutes. Strain, pushing as much of the juice through as possible. Measure 90ml/6 tbsp of the juice, the amount needed, and store the remainder in the fridge. Heat the oil in a wok. Add the chopped onion and fry until golden brown.

2 Add the sugar, stock, fish sauce, dried chillies and the tamarind juice, stirring well until the sugar dissolves. Bring to the boil.

3 Add the prawns, garlic and shallots. Stir-fry until the prawns are cooked, about 3–4 minutes. Garnish with the spring onions.

MEAT & POULTRY
DISHES

Beef Strips with Orange and Ginger

Stir-frying is one of the best ways to cook with the minimum of fat. This recipe is ideal for people trying to lose weight, those requiring a low-fat and low-cholesterol diet or, in fact, anyone who wants to eat healthily.

INGREDIENTS

Serves 4

450g/1lb lean rump, fillet or sirloin steak, cut into thin strips
finely grated rind and juice of 1 orange
15ml/1 tbsp light soy sauce
5ml/1 tsp cornflour
2.5cm/1in fresh root ginger, finely chopped
10ml/2 tsp sesame oil
1 large carrot, cut into matchstick strips
2 spring onions, thinly sliced
rice noodles or boiled rice, to serve

1 Place the steak strips in a bowl and sprinkle over the orange rind and juice. Set aside to marinate for about 30 minutes.

2 Drain the liquid from the steak and reserve. Mix together the steak, soy sauce, cornflour and ginger.

3 Heat the oil in a preheated wok or large frying pan, then add the steak and stir-fry for 1 minute, until lightly coloured. Add the carrot and stir-fry for a further 2–3 minutes.

4 Stir in the spring onions and reserved marinade liquid. Cook, stirring constantly, until boiling and thickened. Serve hot with rice noodles or plain boiled rice.

Sesame Steak

Toasted sesame seeds bring their distinctive smoky aroma to this scrumptious oriental marinade.

INGREDIENTS

Serves 4

450g/1lb rump steak
30ml/2 tbsp sesame seeds
15ml/1 tbsp sesame oil
30ml/2 tbsp vegetable oil
115g/4oz small mushrooms, quartered
1 large green pepper, seeded and cut into strips
4 spring onions, chopped diagonally
boiled rice, to serve

For the marinade

10ml/2 tsp cornflour
30ml/2 tbsp Chinese rice wine or dry sherry
15ml/1 tbsp lemon juice
15ml/1 tbsp soy sauce
few drops of Tabasco sauce
2.5cm/1in fresh root ginger, grated
1 garlic clove, crushed

1 Trim the steak and cut into thin strips about 1 x 5cm/½ x 2in.

2 Make the marinade. In a bowl, blend the cornflour with the rice wine or dry sherry, then stir in the lemon juice, soy sauce, Tabasco sauce, ginger and garlic. Stir in the steak strips, cover and leave in a cool place for 3–4 hours.

3 Place the sesame seeds in a wok or large frying pan and dry-fry over a moderate heat, shaking the pan, until the seeds are golden. Set aside.

4 Heat the sesame and vegetable oils in the wok or frying pan. Drain the steak, reserving the marinade, and stir-fry a few pieces at a time until browned. Remove with a slotted spoon.

5 Add the mushrooms and green pepper and stir-fry for 2–3 minutes. Add the spring onions and cook for 1 minute more.

6 Return the steak to the wok or frying pan, together with the reserved marinade, and stir over a moderate heat for a further 2 minutes until the ingredients are evenly coated with glaze. Sprinkle over the sesame seeds and serve immediately with boiled rice.

── COOK'S TIP ──

This marinade would also be good with pork or chicken.

Chilli Beef with Basil

This is a dish for chilli lovers! It is very easy to prepare – all you need is a wok.

INGREDIENTS

Serves 2

about 90ml/6 tbsp groundnut oil
16–20 large fresh basil leaves
275g/10oz rump steak
30ml/2 tbsp Thai fish sauce (*nam pla*)
5ml/1 tsp dark brown soft sugar
1–2 fresh red chillies, sliced into rings
3 garlic cloves, chopped
5ml/1 tsp chopped fresh root ginger
1 shallot, thinly sliced
30ml/2 tbsp finely chopped fresh basil
 leaves, plus extra to garnish
squeeze of lemon juice
salt and ground black pepper
Thai jasmine rice, to serve

1 Heat the oil in a wok and, when hot, add the whole basil leaves and fry for about 1 minute until crisp and golden. Drain on kitchen paper. Remove the wok from the heat and pour off all but 30ml/2 tbsp of the oil.

--- COOK'S TIP ---

Although not so familiar to western cooks, Thai fish sauce is as widely used in Thai cooking as soy sauce is in Chinese cuisine. In fact, they are not dissimilar in appearance and taste. Called *nam pla*, Thai fish sauce is available at oriental food stores, but if you cannot get it, soy sauce is an adequate substitute.

2 Cut the steak across the grain into thin strips. Mix together the fish sauce and sugar in a bowl. Add the beef, mix well, then leave to marinate for about 30 minutes.

3 Reheat the oil until hot, add the chilli, garlic, ginger and shallot and stir-fry for 30 seconds. Add the beef and chopped basil, then stir-fry for about 3 minutes. Flavour with lemon juice and salt and pepper to taste.

4 Transfer to a warmed serving plate, scatter over the basil leaves to garnish and serve immediately with Thai jasmine rice.

Beef and Aubergine Curry

INGREDIENTS

Serves 6

120ml/4fl oz/½ cup sunflower oil
2 onions, thinly sliced
2.5cm/1in fresh root ginger, sliced and cut in matchsticks
1 garlic clove, crushed
2 fresh red chillies, seeded and very finely sliced
2.5cm/1in fresh turmeric, peeled and crushed, or 5ml/1 tsp ground turmeric
1 lemon grass stem, lower part sliced finely, top bruised
675g/1½ lb braising steak, cut in even-size strips
400ml/14fl oz can coconut milk
300ml/½ pint/1¼ cups water
1 aubergine, sliced and patted dry
5ml/1 tsp tamarind pulp, soaked in 60ml/4 tbsp warm water
salt and freshly ground black pepper
finely sliced chilli, (optional) and Deep-fried Onions, to garnish
boiled rice, to serve

1 Heat half the oil and fry the onions, ginger and garlic until they give off a rich aroma. Add the chillies, turmeric and the lower part of the lemon grass. Push to one side and then turn up the heat and add the steak, stirring until the meat changes colour.

COOK'S TIP

If you want to make this curry, *Gulai Terung Dengan Daging,* ahead, prepare to the end of step 2 and finish later.

2 Add the coconut milk, water, lemon grass top and seasoning to taste. Cover and simmer gently for 1½ hours, or until the meat is tender.

3 Towards the end of the cooking time heat the remaining oil in a frying pan. Fry the aubergine slices until brown on both sides.

4 Add the browned aubergine slices to the beef curry and cook for a further 15 minutes. Stir gently from time to time. Strain the tamarind and stir the juice into the curry. Taste and adjust the seasoning. Put into a warm serving dish. Garnish with the sliced chilli, if using, and Deep-fried Onions, and serve with boiled rice.

Savoury Pork Ribs with Snake Beans

This is a rich and pungent dish. If snake beans are hard to find, you can substitute fine green or runner beans.

INGREDIENTS

Serves 4–6
675g/1½lb pork spare ribs or belly
   of pork
30ml/2 tbsp vegetable oil
120ml/4fl oz/½ cup water
15ml/1 tbsp palm sugar
15ml/1 tbsp fish sauce
150g/5oz snake beans, cut into
   5cm/2in lengths
2 kaffir lime leaves, finely sliced
2 red chillies, finely sliced, to garnish

For the chilli paste
3 dried red chillies, seeded and soaked
4 shallots, chopped
4 garlic cloves, chopped
5ml/1 tsp chopped galangal
1 stalk lemon grass, chopped
6 black peppercorns
5ml/1 tsp shrimp paste
30ml/2 tbsp dried shrimp, rinsed

1 Put all the ingredients for the chilli paste in a mortar and grind together with a pestle until it forms a thick paste.

2 Slice and chop the spare ribs (or belly pork) into 4cm/1½in lengths.

3 Heat the oil in a wok or frying pan. Add the pork and fry for about 5 minutes, until lightly browned.

4 Stir in the chilli paste and continue to cook for another 5 minutes, stirring constantly to stop the paste from sticking to the pan.

5 Add the water, cover and simmer for 7–10 minutes or until the spare ribs are tender. Season with palm sugar and fish sauce.

6 Mix in the snake beans and kaffir lime leaves and fry until the beans are cooked. Serve garnished with sliced red chillies.

Chinese Sweet-and-sour Pork

Sweet-and-sour pork must be one of the most popular dishes served in Chinese restaurants and take-aways in the Western world. Unfortunately, it is often spoiled by cooks who use too much tomato ketchup in the sauce. Here is a classic recipe from Canton, the city of its origin.

INGREDIENTS

Serves 4
350g/12oz lean pork
1.5ml/¼ tsp salt
2.5ml/½ tsp ground Szechuan peppercorns
15ml/1 tbsp Chinese rice wine or dry sherry
115g/4oz bamboo shoots
30ml/2 tbsp plain flour
1 egg, lightly beaten
vegetable oil, for deep-frying

For the sauce
15ml/1 tbsp vegetable oil
1 garlic clove, finely chopped
1 spring onion, cut into short sections
1 small green pepper, seeded and diced
1 fresh red chilli, seeded and thinly shredded
15ml/1 tbsp light soy sauce
30ml/2 tbsp light brown sugar
30–45ml/2–3 tbsp rice vinegar
15ml/1 tbsp tomato purée
about 120ml/4fl oz/½ cup water

1 Cut the pork into small bite-sized cubes and place in a shallow dish. Add the salt, peppercorns and rice wine or dry sherry and set aside to marinate for 15–20 minutes.

2 Drain the bamboo shoots, if canned, and cut them into small cubes the same size as the pork.

3 Dust the pork with flour, dip in the beaten egg and coat with more flour. Heat the oil in a preheated wok and deep-fry the pork in moderately hot oil for 3–4 minutes, stirring to separate the pieces. Remove and drain.

4 Reheat the oil until hot, return the pork to the wok and add the bamboo shoots. Fry for about 1 minute, or until the pork is golden. Remove and drain well.

5 To make the sauce, heat the oil in a clean wok or frying pan and add the garlic, spring onion, green pepper and red chilli. Stir-fry for 30–40 seconds, then add the soy sauce, sugar, rice vinegar, tomato purée and stock or water. Bring to the boil, then add the pork and bamboo shoots. Heat through and stir to mix, then serve.

Twice-cooked Pork – Szechuan Style

This delicious dish is typical of the cuisine of western China.

INGREDIENTS

Serves 4

225g/8oz pork shoulder
1 small green pepper, seeded
115g/4oz sliced bamboo shoots, rinsed
 and drained
1 spring onion
45ml/3 tbsp vegetable oil
2.5ml/½ tsp light brown sugar
15ml/1 tbsp yellow bean sauce
5ml/1 tsp chilli bean sauce
15ml/1 tbsp Chinese rice wine or dry sherry
salt

1 Immerse the pork in a large pan of boiling water, return to the boil and skim the surface. Reduce the heat, cover and simmer for 25–30 minutes. Turn off the heat and leave the pork in the water, covered, to cool, for at least 3–4 hours before removing it from the pan.

2 Trim off any excess fat from the pork and cut the meat into small, very thin slices. Cut the pepper into pieces the same size as the bamboo shoots and cut the spring onion into short sections.

3 Heat the oil in a preheated wok, add the green pepper, spring onion and bamboo shoots and stir-fry for about 1 minute.

4 Add the pork, followed by the sugar, yellow bean sauce, chilli bean sauce and Chinese rice wine or sherry. Season to taste with salt and stir-fry for 1–2 minutes. Transfer to a warm serving dish and serve immediately.

Balti Lamb Tikka

One of the best ways of tenderizing meat is to marinate it in papaya, which must be unripe or it will lend too much sweetness to what should be a savoury dish. Papaya, also known as pawpaw, is readily available from most large supermarkets.

INGREDIENTS

Serves 4

675g/1½lb lean lamb, cubed
1 unripe papaya
45ml/3 tbsp natural yogurt
5ml/1 tsp ginger pulp
5ml/1 tsp chilli powder
5ml/1 tsp garlic pulp
1.5ml/¼ tsp ground turmeric
10ml/2 tsp ground coriander
5ml/1 tsp ground cumin
30ml/2 tbsp lemon juice
15ml/1 tbsp chopped fresh coriander,
   plus extra for garnishing
1.5ml/¼ tsp red food colouring
300ml/½ pint/1¼ cups corn oil
salt
lemon wedges and onion rings,
   to garnish
raita and naan, to serve

1 Place the cubed lamb in a large mixing bowl. Peel the papaya, cut in half and scoop out the seeds. Cut the flesh into cubes, place in a food processor or blender and blend until it is pulped, adding about 15ml/1 tbsp water if necessary.

COOK'S TIP

A good-quality meat tenderizer, available from supermarkets, can be used in place of the papaya. However, the meat will need a longer marinating time and should ideally be left to tenderize overnight.

2 Pour about 30ml/2 tbsp of the papaya pulp over the lamb cubes and rub it in well with your fingers. Set aside to marinate for at least 3 hours.

3 Meanwhile, mix together the yogurt, ginger, chilli powder, garlic, turmeric, ground coriander, cumin, lemon juice, fresh coriander, red food colouring and 30ml/2 tbsp of the oil. Season with salt and set aside.

4 Spoon the yogurt mixture over the lamb and mix together well.

5 Heat the remaining oil in a wok. When it is hot, lower the heat slightly and add the lamb cubes, a few at a time. Deep fry the batches of lamb for 5–7 minutes or until the lamb is cooked and tender. Transfer each batch to a warmed serving dish and keep warm while you cook the next batch.

6 When all the batches of lamb have been cooked, garnish with the lemon wedges, onion rings and fresh coriander. Serve with raita and naan.

Spiced Lamb with Spinach

INGREDIENTS

Serves 3–4

45ml/3 tbsp vegetable oil
500g/1¼lb lean boneless lamb, cut into
  2.5cm/1in cubes
1 onion, chopped
3 garlic cloves, finely chopped
1cm/½in fresh root ginger,
  finely chopped
6 black peppercorns
4 whole cloves
1 bay leaf
3 green cardamom pods, crushed
5ml/1 tsp ground cumin
5ml/1 tsp ground coriander
generous pinch of cayenne pepper
150ml/¼ pint/⅔ cup water
2 tomatoes, peeled, seeded
  and chopped
5ml/1 tsp salt
400g/14oz fresh spinach, trimmed,
  washed and finely chopped
5ml/1 tsp garam masala
crisp-fried onions and fresh coriander
  sprigs, to garnish
naan bread or spiced basmati rice, to
  serve

1 Heat a wok until hot. Add 30ml/
2 tbsp of the oil and swirl it
around. When hot, stir-fry the lamb in
batches until evenly browned. Remove
the lamb and set aside. Add the
remaining oil, onion, garlic and ginger
and stir-fry for 2–3 minutes.

2 Add the peppercorns, cloves, bay
leaf, cardamom pods, cumin,
ground coriander and cayenne pepper.
Stir-fry for 30–45 seconds. Return the
lamb and add the water, tomatoes and
salt and bring to the boil. Simmer,
covered over a very low heat for about
1 hour, stirring occasionally until the
meat is cooked and tender.

3 Increase the heat, then gradually
add the spinach to the lamb,
stirring to mix. Keep stirring and
cooking until the spinach wilts
completely and most, but not all, of the
liquid has evaporated and you are left
with a thick green sauce. Stir in the
garam masala. Garnish with crisp-fried
onions and coriander sprigs. Serve with
naan bread or spiced basmati rice.

Paper-thin Lamb with Spring Onions

Spring onions lend a delicious flavour to the lamb in this simple supper dish.

INGREDIENTS

Serves 3–4
450g/1lb lamb neck fillet
30ml/2 tbsp Chinese rice wine or
  dry sherry
10ml/2 tsp light soy sauce
2.5ml/½ tsp roasted and ground
  Szechuan peppercorns
2.5ml/½ tsp salt
2.5ml/½ tsp dark brown soft sugar
20ml/4 tsp dark soy sauce
15ml/1 tbsp sesame oil
30ml/2 tbsp groundnut oil
2 garlic cloves, thinly sliced
2 bunches spring onions, cut into
  7.5cm/3 in lengths, then shredded
30ml/2 tbsp chopped fresh coriander

1 Wrap the lamb and place in the freezer for about 1 hour until just frozen. Cut the meat across the grain into paper-thin slices. Put the lamb slices in a bowl, add 10ml/2 tsp of the rice wine or sherry, the soy sauce and ground Szechuan peppercorns. Mix well and set aside to marinate for 15–30 minutes.

COOK'S TIP

Some large supermarkets sell very thinly sliced lean lamb ready for stir-frying, which makes this dish even quicker to prepare.

2 Make the sauce: in a bowl mix together the remaining rice wine or sherry, the salt, brown sugar, soy sauce and 10ml/2 tsp of the sesame oil. Set aside.

3 Heat the groundnut oil in a preheated wok. Add the garlic and let it sizzle for a few seconds, then add the lamb. Stir-fry for about 1 minute, until the lamb is no longer pink. Pour in the sauce and stir briefly to mix.

4 Add the spring onions and coriander and stir-fry for 15–20 seconds, until the spring onions just wilt. The finished dish should be slightly dry in appearance. Serve at once, sprinkled with the remaining sesame oil.

Spiced Chicken Stir-fry

INGREDIENTS

Serves 4

1.5kg/3–3½lb chicken, cut in 8 pieces
5ml/1 tsp each salt and freshly ground
   black pepper
2 garlic cloves, crushed
150ml/¼ pint/⅔ cup sunflower oil

For the sauce

25g/1oz butter
30ml/2 tbsp sunflower oil
1 onion, sliced
4 garlic cloves, crushed
2 large, ripe beefsteak tomatoes, sliced
   and chopped, or 400g/14oz can
   chopped tomatoes with
   chilli, drained
600ml/1 pint/2½ cups water
50ml/2fl oz/¼ cup dark soy sauce
salt and freshly ground black pepper
sliced fresh red chilli, to garnish
Deep-fried Onions, to
   garnish (optional)
boiled rice, to serve

1 Preheat the oven to 190°C/375°F/ Gas 5. Make two slashes in the fleshy part of each chicken piece. Rub well with the salt, pepper and garlic. Drizzle with a little of the oil and bake for 30 minutes, or shallow-fry, in hot oil for 12–15 minutes, until brown.

2 To make the sauce, heat the butter and oil in a wok and fry the onion and garlic until soft. Add the tomatoes, water, soy sauce and seasoning. Boil briskly for 5 minutes, to reduce the sauce and concentrate the flavour.

3 Add the chicken to the sauce in the wok. Turn the chicken pieces over in the sauce to coat them well. Continue cooking slowly for about 20 minutes until the chicken pieces are tender. Stir the mixture occasionally.

4 Arrange the chicken on a warm serving platter and garnish with the sliced chilli and Deep-fried Onions, if using. Serve with boiled rice.

Stir-fried Chicken with Pineapple

INGREDIENTS

Serves 4–6

500g/1¼ lb boneless, skinless chicken
   breasts, thinly sliced at an angle
30ml/2 tbsp cornflour
60ml/4 tbsp sunflower oil
1 garlic clove, crushed
5cm/2in fresh root ginger, peeled and
   cut in matchsticks
1 small onion, thinly sliced
1 fresh pineapple, peeled, cored and
   cubed, or 425g/15oz can pineapple
   chunks in natural juice
30ml/2 tbsp dark soy sauce or
   15ml/1 tbsp *kecap manis*
1 bunch spring onions, white bulbs left
   whole, green tops sliced
salt and freshly ground black pepper

1 Toss the strips of chicken in the cornflour with a little seasoning. Fry in hot oil until tender.

2 Lift out of the wok or frying pan and keep warm. Reheat the oil and fry the garlic, ginger and onion until soft, but not browned. Add the fresh pineapple and 120ml/4fl oz/½ cup water, or the canned pineapple pieces together with their juice.

3 Stir in the soy sauce or *kecap manis* and return the chicken to the pan to heat through.

4 Taste and adjust the seasoning. Stir in the whole spring onion bulbs and half of the sliced green tops. Toss well together and then turn the chicken stir-fry on to a serving platter. Serve garnished with the remaining sliced green spring onions.

Khara Masala Balti Chicken

Whole spices – *khara* – are used in this recipe, giving it a wonderfully rich flavour. This is a dry dish, so it is best served with raita and paratha.

INGREDIENTS

Serves 4

3 curry leaves
1.5ml/¼ tsp mustard seeds
1.5ml/¼ tsp fennel seeds
1.5ml/¼ tsp onion seeds
2.5ml/½ tsp crushed dried red chillies
2.5ml/½ tsp white cumin seeds
1.5ml/¼ tsp fenugreek seeds
2.5ml/½ tsp crushed pomegranate seeds
5ml/1tsp salt
5ml/1 tsp shredded ginger
3 garlic cloves, sliced
60ml/4 tbsp corn oil
4 fresh green chillies, slit
1 large onion, sliced
1 medium tomato, sliced
675g/1½lb chicken, skinned, boned and cubed
15 ml/1 tbsp chopped fresh coriander, to garnish
paratha, to serve

1 Mix together the curry leaves, mustard seeds, fennel seeds, onion seeds, crushed red chillies, cumin seeds, fenugreek seeds and crushed pomegranate seeds in a large bowl. Add the salt.

2 Add the shredded ginger and garlic cloves to the bowl.

3 Heat the oil in a preheated wok. When the oil is hot, add the spice mixture, then the green chillies.

4 Add the onion to the wok and stir-fry over a medium heat for 5–7 minutes.

5 Add the tomato and chicken pieces to the wok and cook over a medium heat for about 7 minutes or until the chicken is cooked through and the sauce has reduced slightly.

6 Stir the mixture over the heat for a further 3–5 minutes, then garnish with the chopped fresh coriander and serve with the paratha.

Szechuan Chicken

A wok is the ideal cooking pot for this stir-fried chicken dish. The flavours emerge wonderfully and the chicken is fresh and crisp.

INGREDIENTS

Serves 4

350g/12oz chicken thigh, boned and skinned
1.5ml/¼ tsp salt
½ egg white, lightly beaten
10ml/2 tsp cornflour paste
1 green pepper, cored and seeded
60ml/4 tbsp vegetable oil
3–4 whole dried red chillies, soaked in water for 10 minutes
1 spring onion, cut into short sections
few small pieces of fresh root ginger, peeled
15ml/1 tbsp sweet bean paste or hoi-sin sauce
5ml/1 tsp chilli bean paste
15ml/1 tbsp Chinese rice wine or dry sherry
115g/4oz roasted cashew nuts
few drops sesame oil

1 Cut the chicken meat into small cubes, each about the size of a sugar lump. Mix together the chicken, salt, egg white and cornflour paste in a bowl.

2 Cut the green pepper into cubes about the same size as the chicken.

3 Heat the oil in a preheated wok. Stir-fry the chicken cubes for about 1 minute, or until the colour changes. Remove from the wok with a slotted spoon and keep warm.

4 Add the green pepper, chillies, spring onion and ginger and stir-fry for about 1 minute. Then add the chicken, sweet bean paste or hoi-sin sauce, chilli bean paste and rice wine or sherry. Blend well and cook for 1 minute more. Finally add the cashew nuts and sesame oil. Serve hot.

Green Curry Coconut Chicken

The recipe given here for green curry paste takes time to make properly. Pork, prawns and fish can all be used instead of chicken, but cooking times must be adjusted accordingly.

INGREDIENTS

Serves 4–6

1.1kg/2½lb chicken
600ml/1 pint/2½ cups canned coconut milk
450ml/¾ pint/1¾ cups chicken stock
2 kaffir lime leaves
350g/12oz sweet potatoes, roughly chopped
350g/12oz winter squash, seeded and roughly chopped
115g/4oz French beans, halved
1 small bunch fresh coriander, shredded, to garnish

For the green curry paste
10ml/2 tsp coriander seeds
2.5ml/½ tsp caraway or cumin seeds
3–4 medium fresh green chillies, finely chopped
20ml/4 tsp sugar
10ml/2 tsp salt
7.5cm/3in lemon grass
2cm/¾in galangal or fresh root ginger, finely chopped
3 garlic cloves, crushed
4 shallots or 1 medium onion, finely chopped
2cm/¾in square shrimp paste
45ml/3 tbsp finely chopped fresh coriander
45ml/3 tbsp finely chopped fresh mint
2.5ml/½ tsp ground nutmeg
30ml/2 tbsp vegetable oil

1 To prepare the chicken, remove the legs, then separate the thighs from the drumsticks. Separate the lower part of the chicken carcass by cutting through the rib section with kitchen scissors. Divide the breast part in half down the middle, then chop each half in two. Remove the skin from all the pieces and discard.

2 Strain the coconut milk into a bowl, reserving the thick part. Place the chicken in a stainless steel or enamel saucepan, pour in the thin part of the coconut milk and the stock. Add the lime leaves and simmer, uncovered, for 40 minutes. Remove the chicken from the saucepan and allow to cool. Reserve the cooking liquid. Remove the cooled meat from the bone and set aside.

3 To make the curry paste, dry-fry the coriander seeds and caraway or cumin seeds. Grind the chillies with the sugar and salt in a mortar with a pestle to make a smooth paste. Combine the seeds from the wok with the chilli paste, the lemon grass, galangal or ginger, garlic and shallots or onion, then grind smoothly. Add the shrimp paste, coriander leaves, mint, nutmeg and vegetable oil.

4 Place 250ml/8fl oz/1 cup of the reserved cooking liquid in a large wok. Add 60–75ml/4–5 tbsp of the curry paste to the liquid, according to taste. Boil rapidly until the liquid has reduced completely. Add the chicken stock, chicken meat, sweet potatoes, squash and beans. Simmer for 10–15 minutes until the potatoes are cooked. Stir in the thick part of the coconut milk and simmer gently to thicken. Serve garnished with coriander.

Balti Baby Chicken in Tamarind Sauce

The tamarind in this recipe gives the dish a sweet and sour flavour; this is also quite a hot Balti.

Ingredients

Serves 4–6

60ml/4 tbsp tomato ketchup
15ml/1 tbsp tamarind paste
60ml/4 tbsp water
7.5ml/1½ tsp chilli powder
7.5ml/1½ tsp salt
15ml/1 tbsp sugar
7.5ml/1½ tsp ginger pulp
7.5ml/1½ tsp garlic pulp
30ml/2 tbsp desiccated coconut
30ml/2 tbsp sesame seeds
5ml/1 tsp poppy seeds
5ml/1 tsp ground cumin
7.5ml/1½ tsp ground coriander
2 x 450g/1lb baby chickens, skinned
  and cut into 6–8 pieces
75ml/5 tbsp corn oil
120ml/8 tbsp curry leaves
2.5ml/½ tsp onion seeds
3 large dried red chillies
2.5ml/½ tsp fenugreek seeds
10–12 cherry tomatoes
45ml/3 tbsp chopped fresh coriander
2 fresh green chillies, chopped

1 Put the tomato ketchup, tamarind paste and water into a large mixing bowl and blend together with a fork.

2 Add the chilli powder, salt, sugar, ginger, garlic, coconut, sesame seeds, poppy seeds, ground cumin and ground coriander to the mixture.

3 Add the chicken pieces to the bowl and stir until they are well coated with the spice mixture. Set aside.

4 Heat the oil in a preheated wok. When it is hot, add the curry leaves, onion seeds, dried red chillies and fenugreek seeds and fry for 1 minute.

5 Lower the heat to medium and add the chicken pieces, together with their sauce, 2 or 3 pieces at a time. When all the chicken has been added to the wok, stir to mix well.

6 Simmer gently for 12–15 minutes or until the chicken is thoroughly cooked through.

7 Add the tomatoes, fresh coriander and green chillies to the wok and serve immediately.

Indonesian-style Satay Chicken

Satay traditionally forms part of a *Rijsttafel* – literally rice table – a vast feast of as many as 40 different dishes served with a large bowl of plain rice. However, for the less ambitious, creamy coconut satay makes these chicken pieces a mouth-watering dish to present at the table at any time of the day.

INGREDIENTS

Serves 4

50g/2oz raw peanuts
45ml/3 tbsp vegetable oil
1 small onion, finely chopped
2.5cm/1in fresh root ginger, peeled and
    finely chopped
1 clove garlic, crushed
675g/1¹/₂lb chicken thighs, skinned and
    cut into cubes
90g/3¹/₂oz creamed coconut,
    roughly chopped
15ml/1 tbsp chilli sauce
60ml/4 tbsp crunchy peanut butter
5ml/1 tsp soft dark brown sugar
150ml/¹/₄ pint/²/₃ cup milk
1.5ml/¹/₄ tsp salt

1 Shell the peanuts and remove the skins by rubbing them between the palms of the hands. Put them in a small bowl, add just enough water to cover and soak for 1 minute. Drain the nuts and cut them into slivers.

2 Heat the wok and add 5ml/1 tsp oil. When the oil is hot, stir-fry the peanuts for 1 minute until crisp and golden. Remove with a slotted spoon and drain on kitchen paper.

3 Add the remaining oil to the hot wok. When the oil is hot, add the onion, ginger and garlic and stir-fry for 2–3 minutes until softened but not browned. Remove with a slotted spoon and drain on kitchen paper.

— COOK'S TIP —

Soak bamboo skewers in cold water for at least 2 hours, or preferably overnight, so that they do not char when keeping the threaded chicken warm in the oven.

4 Add the chicken pieces to the wok and stir-fry for 3–4 minutes until crisp and golden on all sides. Thread on to pre-soaked bamboo skewers and keep warm.

5 Add the creamed coconut to the hot wok in small pieces and stir-fry until melted. Add the chilli sauce, peanut butter and ginger mixture and simmer for 2 minutes. Stir in the sugar, milk and salt, and simmer for a further 3 minutes. Serve the skewered chicken hot, with a dish of the hot dipping sauce sprinkled with the roasted peanuts.

Balti Chicken with Lentils

This is rather an unusual combination of flavours, but it is certainly worth trying! The mango powder gives a delicious tangy flavour to this spicy dish.

INGREDIENTS

Serves 4–6

75g/3oz split yellow lentils
60ml/4 tbsp corn oil
2 medium leeks, chopped
6 large dried red chillies
4 curry leaves
5ml/1 tsp mustard seeds
10ml/2 tsp mango powder
2 medium tomatoes, chopped
2.5ml/½ tsp chilli powder
5ml/1 tsp ground coriander
450g/1lb boneless chicken, skinned
  and cubed
salt
15ml/1 tbsp chopped fresh coriander,
  to garnish
paratha, to serve

1 Put the lentils in a sieve and wash carefully under plenty of cold running water.

2 Put the lentils in a saucepan and add just enough water to cover. Bring to the boil and cook for 10 minutes or until they are soft but not mushy. Drain thoroughly, transfer to a bowl mead and set aside.

3 Heat the oil in a pre-heated wok until hot. Lower the heat and add the leeks, dried red chillies, curry leaves and mustard seeds and stir-fry gently for 2–3 minutes.

4 Add the mango powder, tomatoes, chilli powder, ground coriander and chicken. Season with salt and stir-fry for 7–10 minutes.

COOK'S TIP

Split yellow lentils, known as chana dhal, are available from Asian stores. However, if you cannot get them, split yellow peas are a good substitute.

5 Mix in the cooked lentils and fry for a further 2 minutes or until the chicken is cooked through.

6 Garnish with fresh coriander and serve immediately with paratha.

Thai Stir-fry Chicken Curry

Here chicken and potatoes are simmered in a wok filled with coconut milk, one of the essential ingredients of Thai cuisine. The end result is a superb flavoursome curry.

INGREDIENTS

Serves 4

1 onion
15ml/1 tbsp groundnut oil
400ml/14fl oz/1²/₃ cups coconut milk
30ml/2 tbsp red curry paste
30ml/2 tbsp Thai fish sauce (*nam pla*)
15ml/1 tbsp soft light brown sugar
225g/8oz tiny new potatoes
450g/1lb skinless chicken breasts, cut into chunks
15ml/1 tbsp lime juice
30ml/2 tbsp chopped fresh mint
15ml/1 tbsp chopped fresh basil
salt and ground black pepper
2 kaffir lime leaves, shredded and 1–2 fresh red chillies, seeded and finely shredded, to garnish

1 Cut the onion into wedges, using a sharp knife.

COOK'S TIP

You can use boneless chicken thighs instead of breasts. Simply skin them, cut the flesh into chunks and cook in the coconut milk with the potatoes.

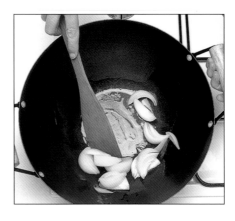

2 Heat a wok until hot, add the oil and swirl it around. Add the onion and stir-fry for 3–4 minutes.

3 Pour in the coconut milk, then bring to the boil, stirring. Stir in the curry paste, fish sauce and sugar.

4 Add the potatoes and seasoning, cover and simmer gently for about 20 minutes.

5 Add the chicken chunks, cover and cook over a low heat for a further 10–15 minutes, until the chicken and potatoes are tender.

6 Stir in the lime juice, chopped mint and basil. Serve at once, sprinkled with the shredded kaffir lime leaves and red chillies.

Duck and Ginger Chop Suey

Chicken can also be used in this recipe, but duck gives a richer contrast of flavours.

INGREDIENTS

Serves 4

2 duck breasts, about 175g/6oz each
45ml/3 tbsp sunflower oil
1 small egg, lightly beaten
1 garlic clove
175g/6oz beansprouts
2 slices fresh root ginger, cut into matchsticks
10ml/2 tsp oyster sauce
2 spring onions, cut into matchsticks
salt and ground black pepper

For the marinade

15ml/1 tbsp clear honey
10ml/2 tsp Chinese rice wine or dry sherry
10ml/2 tsp light soy sauce
10ml/2 tsp dark soy sauce

1 Remove the fat and skin from the duck, cut the breasts into thin strips and place in a bowl. Mix the marinade ingredients together, pour over the duck, cover, chill and marinate overnight.

2 Next day, make the egg omelette. Heat a small frying pan and add 15ml/1 tbsp of the oil. When the oil is hot, pour in the egg and swirl around to make an omelette. Once cooked, leave it to cool and then cut into strips. Drain the duck and discard the marinade.

3 Bruise the garlic with the flat blade of a knife. Heat 10ml/2 tsp of the oil in a preheated wok. When the oil is hot, add the garlic and fry for 30 seconds, pressing it to release the flavour. Discard. Add the beansprouts with seasoning and stir-fry for 30 seconds. Transfer to a heated dish, draining off any liquid.

4 Heat the remaining oil in a preheated wok. When the oil is hot, stir-fry the duck for 3 minutes until cooked. Add the ginger and oyster sauce and stir-fry for a further 2 minutes. Add the beansprouts, egg strips and spring onions, stir-fry briefly and serve.

Duck with Chinese Mushrooms and Ginger

Ducks are often seen, comically herded in single file, along the water channels between the rice paddies throughout the country. The substantial Chinese population in Indonesia is particularly fond of duck and the delicious ingredients in this recipe give it an oriental flavour.

INGREDIENTS

Serves 4

2.5kg/5½lb duck
5ml/1 tsp sugar
50ml/2fl oz/¼ cup light soy sauce
2 garlic cloves, crushed
8 dried Chinese mushrooms, soaked in 350ml/12fl oz/1½ cups warm water for 15 minutes
1 onion, sliced
5cm/2in fresh root ginger, sliced and cut in matchsticks
200g/7oz baby sweetcorn
½ bunch spring onions, white bulbs left whole, green tops sliced
15–30ml/1–2 tbsp cornflour, mixed to a paste with 60ml/4 tbsp water
salt and freshly ground black pepper
boiled rice, to serve

1 Cut the duck along the breast, open it up and cut along each side of the backbone. Use the backbone, wings and giblets to make a stock, to use later in the recipe. Any trimmings of fat can be rendered in a frying pan, to use later in the recipe. Cut each leg and each breast in half. Place in a bowl, rub with the sugar and then pour over the soy sauce and garlic.

2 Drain the mushrooms, reserving the soaking liquid. Trim and discard the stalks.

3 Fry the onion and ginger in the duck fat, in a frying pan, until they give off a good aroma. Push to one side. Lift the duck pieces out of the soy sauce and fry them until browned. Add the mushrooms and reserved liquid.

4 Add 600ml/1 pint/2½ cups of the duck stock or water to the browned duck pieces. Season, cover and cook over a gentle heat for about 1 hour, until the duck is tender.

5 Add the sweetcorn and the white part of the spring onions and cook for a further 10 minutes. Remove from the heat and add the cornflour paste. Return to the heat and bring to the boil, stirring. Cook for 1 minute until glossy. Serve, scattered with the spring onion tops, with boiled rice.

VARIATION

Replace the corn with chopped celery and slices of drained, canned water chestnuts.

VEGETABLES &
VEGETARIAN
DISHES

Aubergine in Spicy Sauce

Aubergines are given a royal treatment in this recipe, where they are stir-fried with seasonings more commonly associated with fish cooking.

INGREDIENTS

Serves 4

450g/1lb aubergines
3–4 whole dried red chillies, soaked in
    water for 10 minutes
vegetable oil, for deep frying
1 clove garlic, finely chopped
5ml/1 tsp finely chopped fresh ginger
5ml/1 tsp finely chopped spring onion,
    white part only
115g/4oz lean pork, thinly
    shredded (optional)
15ml/1 tbsp light soy sauce
15ml/1 tbsp light brown sugar
15ml/1 tbsp chilli bean sauce
15ml/1 tbsp Chinese rice wine or
    dry sherry
15ml/1 tbsp rice vinegar
10ml/2 tsp cornflour paste, see page 30
5ml/1 tsp finely chopped spring
    onions, green part only, to garnish
few drops sesame oil

1 Cut the aubergines into short strips the size of chips – the skin can either be peeled off or left on, whichever you prefer. Cut the soaked red chillies into two or three small pieces and discard the seeds.

2 Heat the oil in a preheated wok and deep fry the aubergine chips for about 3–4 minutes or until limp. Remove and drain.

3 Pour off the excess oil, leaving about 15ml/1 tbsp in the wok. Add the garlic, ginger, white spring onions and chillies, stir a few times, then add the pork, if using. Stir-fry the meat for about 1 minute or until it becomes pale, almost white, in colour. Add all the seasonings, then increase the heat and bring the mixture to the boil.

4 Add the aubergines to the wok, blend well and braise for 30–40 seconds, then thicken the sauce with the cornflour paste, stirring until smooth. Garnish with the green spring onions and sprinkle with sesame oil.

--- COOK'S TIP ---

Soaking dried chillies in water will reduce their spicy flavour. If you prefer a milder chilli taste, soak for longer than the recommended 10 minutes.

Spiced Coconut Mushrooms

Here is a simple and delicious way to cook mushrooms. They can be served with almost any oriental meal as well as with traditional western grilled or roasted meats and poultry.

INGREDIENTS

Serves 4
30ml/2 tbsp groundnut oil
2 garlic cloves, finely chopped
2 fresh red chillies, seeded and sliced
  into rings
3 shallots, finely chopped
225g/8oz brown-cap mushrooms,
  thickly sliced
150ml/¼ pint/⅔ cup coconut milk
30ml/2 tbsp chopped fresh coriander
salt and ground black pepper

1 Heat a wok until hot, add the oil and swirl it round the wok. Add the garlic and chillies, then stir-fry for a few seconds.

COOK'S TIP

Use snipped fresh chives instead of chopped fresh coriander, if you wish.

2 Add the shallots and stir-fry for 2–3 minutes until softened. Add the mushrooms and stir-fry for 3 minutes.

3 Pour in the coconut milk and bring to the boil. Boil rapidly over a high heat until the liquid has reduced by about half and coats the mushrooms. Season to taste with salt and pepper.

4 Sprinkle over the chopped coriander and toss the mushrooms gently to mix. Serve at once.

Spicy Courgette Fritters with Thai Salsa

The Thai salsa goes just as well with plain stir-fried salmon strips or stir-fried beef as it does with these courgette fritters.

INGREDIENTS

Serves 2–4
10ml/2 tsp cumin seeds
10ml/2 tsp coriander seeds
450g/1lb courgettes
115g/4oz chick-pea (gram) flour
2.5ml/½ tsp bicarbonate of soda
120ml/4fl oz/½ cup groundnut oil
salt and ground black pepper
fresh mint sprigs, to garnish

For the Thai salsa
½ cucumber, diced
3 spring onions, chopped
6 radishes, cubed
30ml/2 tbsp fresh mint, chopped
2.5cm/1in fresh root ginger, peeled and grated
45ml/3 tbsp lime juice
30ml/2 tbsp caster sugar
3 cloves garlic, crushed

1 Heat the wok, then dry fry the cumin and coriander seeds. Cool them, then grind well, using a pestle and mortar.

COOK'S TIP

You can substitute mooli, also known as daikon and white radish, for the round radishes in the salsa.

2 Cut the courgettes into 7.5cm/3in sticks. Place in a bowl.

3 Process the flour, bicarbonate of soda, spices and salt and pepper in a food processor or blender. Add 120ml/4fl oz warm water with 15ml/1 tbsp groundnut oil and process again.

4 Coat the courgettes in the batter, then leave to stand for 10 minutes.

5 To make the salsa, mix together the cucumber, spring onions, radishes, mint, ginger and lime juice in a bowl. Stir in the sugar and the garlic.

6 Heat the wok, then add the remaining oil. When the oil is hot, stir-fry the courgettes in batches. Drain well on kitchen paper, then serve hot with the Thai salsa, garnished with fresh mint sprigs.

Spiced Cauliflower Braise

A delicious vegetable stew, known as *Sambal Kol Kembang,* which combines coconut milk with spices and is perfect as a vegetarian main course or as part of a buffet.

INGREDIENTS

Serves 4

1 cauliflower
2 medium or 1 large tomato(es)
1 onion, chopped
2 garlic cloves, crushed
1 fresh green chilli, seeded
2.5ml/½ tsp ground turmeric
1cm/½ in cube *terasi*
30ml/2 tbsp sunflower oil
400ml/14fl oz coconut milk
250ml/8fl oz/1 cup water
5ml/1 tsp sugar
5ml/1 tsp tamarind pulp, soaked in
    45ml/3 tbsp warm water
salt

1 Trim the stalk from the cauliflower and divide into tiny florets. Skin the tomato(es) if liked. Chop the flesh into 1–2.5cm/½–1in pieces.

2 Grind the chopped onion, garlic, green chilli, ground turmeric and *terasi* together to a paste in a food processor or with a pestle and mortar. Heat the sunflower oil in a wok or large frying pan and fry the spice paste to bring out the aromatic flavours, without allowing it to brown.

3 Add the cauliflower florets and toss well to coat in the spices. Stir in the coconut milk, water, sugar and salt to taste. Simmer for 5 minutes. Strain the tamarind and reserve the juice.

4 Add the tamarind juice and chopped tomatoes to the pan then cook for 2–3 minutes only. Taste and check the seasoning and serve.

Spicy Scrambled Eggs

This is a lovely way to liven up scrambled eggs. When making *Orak Arik,* prepare all the ingredients ahead so that the vegetables retain all their crunch and colour.

INGREDIENTS

Serves 4

30ml/2 tbsp sunflower oil
1 onion, finely sliced
225g/8oz Chinese leaves, finely sliced
    or cut in diamonds
200g/7oz can sweetcorn kernels
1 small fresh red chilli, seeded and
    finely sliced (optional)
30ml/2 tbsp water
2 eggs, beaten
salt and freshly ground black pepper
Deep-fried Onions, to garnish

1 Heat a wok, add the oil and fry the onion, until soft but not browned.

2 Add the Chinese leaves and toss well together. Add the sweetcorn, chilli and water. Cover with a lid and cook for 2 minutes.

3 Remove the lid and stir in the beaten eggs and seasoning. Stir constantly until the eggs are creamy and just set. Serve on warmed plates, scattered with crisp Deep-fried Onions.

Spiced Tofu Stir-fry

You could add any quickly cooked vegetable to this stir-fry – try mangetouts, sugar snap peas, leeks or thin slices of carrot.

INGREDIENTS

Serves 4
10ml/2 tsp ground cumin
15ml/1 tbsp paprika
5ml/1 tsp ground ginger
good pinch of cayenne pepper
15ml/1 tbsp caster sugar
275g/10oz firm tofu
oil, for frying
2 garlic cloves, crushed
1 bunch spring onions, sliced
1 red pepper, seeded and sliced
1 yellow pepper, seeded and sliced
225g/8oz brown-cap mushrooms, halved or quartered if very large
1 large courgette, sliced
115g/4oz fine green beans, halved
50g/2oz/½ cup pine nuts
15ml/1 tbsp lime juice
15ml/1 tbsp clear honey
salt and ground black pepper

3 Add a little more oil to the wok or frying pan and stir-fry the garlic and spring onions for 3 minutes. Add the remaining vegetables and stir-fry over a medium heat for 6 minutes, or until beginning to soften and turn golden. Season well.

4 Return the tofu to the pan with the pine nuts, lime juice and honey. Heat through and serve.

1 Mix together the cumin, paprika, ginger, cayenne and sugar with plenty of seasoning. Cut the tofu into cubes and coat them thoroughly in the spice mixture.

2 Heat some oil in a preheated wok or large frying pan. Cook the tofu over a high heat for 3–4 minutes, turning occasionally. Take care not to break up the tofu too much. Remove with a slotted spoon. Wipe out the wok or pan with kitchen paper.

Karahi Shredded Cabbage with Cumin

This cabbage is only lightly spiced and makes a good accompaniment to most other Balti dishes.

INGREDIENTS

Serves 4
15ml/1 tbsp corn oil
50g/2oz butter
2.5ml/½ tsp crushed coriander seeds
2.5ml/½ tsp white cumin seeds
6 dried red chillies
1 small Savoy cabbage, shredded
12 mangetouts
3 fresh red chillies, seeded and sliced
12 baby sweetcorn
salt
25g/1oz flaked almonds, toasted and 15ml/1 tbsp chopped fresh coriander, to garnish

1 Heat the oil and butter in a preheated wok and, when the butter has melted, add the crushed coriander seeds, cumin seeds and dried red chillies.

2 Add the shredded cabbage and mangetouts to the wok and stir-fry for about 5 minutes.

3 Add the fresh red chillies, baby sweetcorn and salt and stir-fry for a further 3 minutes.

4 Garnish the cabbage with toasted almonds and fresh coriander and serve hot.

—— COOK'S TIP ——

Unlike many parts of the Indian sub-continent, Pakistan – whence Balti recipes come – is generally a meat-eating nation. Vegetable dishes are, therefore, usually cooked as side dishes, rather than as a main dish, much in the way they are in the West. Consequently, this delicious, slightly spicy treatment of cabbage would go as well with a traditional western roast as it would with a Balti curry or stir-fry.

Water Spinach with Brown Bean Sauce

Water spinach, often known as Siamese watercress, is a green vegetable with arrowhead-shaped leaves. If you can't find it, use spinach, watercress, pak choy or even broccoli, and adjust the cooking time accordingly. There are excellent variations to this recipe using black bean sauce, shrimp paste or fermented bean curd instead of brown bean sauce.

INGREDIENTS

Serves 4–6
1 bunch water spinach, about
   1kg/2¼lb in weight
45ml/3 tbsp vegetable oil
15ml/1 tbsp chopped garlic
15ml/1 tbsp brown bean sauce
30ml/2 tbsp fish sauce
15ml/1 tbsp granulated sugar
freshly black ground pepper

1 Trim and discard the bottom coarse, woody end of the water spinach. Cut the remaining part into 5cm/2in lengths, keeping the leaves separate from the stems.

2 Heat the oil in a wok or large frying pan. When it starts to smoke, add the chopped garlic and toss for 10 seconds.

3 Add the stem part of the water spinach, let it sizzle and cook for 1 minute, then add the leafy parts.

4 Stir in the brown bean sauce, fish sauce, sugar and pepper. Toss and turn over the spinach until it begins to wilt, about 3–4 minutes. Transfer to a serving dish and serve immediately.

Mixed Vegetables in Coconut Milk

A most delicious way of cooking vegetables. If you don't like highly spiced food, use fewer red chilli peppers.

INGREDIENTS

Serves 4–6
450g/1lb mixed vegetables, such as
   aubergines, baby sweetcorn, carrots,
   snake beans and patty pan squash
8 red chillies, seeded
2 stalks lemon grass, chopped
4 kaffir lime leaves, torn
30ml/2 tbsp vegetable oil
250ml/8fl oz/1 cup coconut milk
30ml/2 tbsp fish sauce
salt
15–20 Thai basil leaves, to garnish

1 Cut the vegetables into similar size shapes using a sharp knife.

2 Put the red chillies, lemon grass and kaffir lime leaves in a mortar and grind together with a pestle.

3 Heat the oil in a wok or large deep frying pan. Add the chilli mixture and fry for 2–3 minutes.

4 Stir in the coconut milk and bring to the boil. Add the vegetables and cook for about 5 minutes or until they are tender. Season with the fish sauce and salt, and garnish with basil leaves.

NOODLE & RICE
DISHES

Thai Noodles with Chinese Chives

This recipe requires a little time for preparation but the cooking time is very fast. Everything is cooked speedily in a hot wok and should be eaten at once.

INGREDIENTS

Serves 4

350g/12oz dried rice noodles
1cm/½ in fresh root ginger, grated
30ml/2 tbsp light soy sauce
45ml/3 tbsp vegetable oil
225g/8oz Quorn, cut into small cubes
2 garlic cloves, crushed
1 large onion, cut into thin wedges
115g/4oz fried tofu, thinly sliced
1 fresh green chilli, seeded and
   finely sliced
175g/6oz beansprouts
115g/4oz Chinese chives, cut into
   5cm/2in lengths
50g/2oz roasted peanuts, ground
30ml/2 tbsp dark soy sauce
fresh coriander leaves, to garnish

1 Place the noodles in a large bowl, cover with warm water and soak for 20–30 minutes, then drain. Blend together the ginger, light soy sauce and 15ml/1 tbsp of the oil in a bowl. Stir in the Quorn and set aside for 10 minutes. Drain, reserving the marinade.

2 Heat 15ml/1 tbsp of the oil in a preheated wok or frying pan and fry the garlic for a few seconds. Add the Quorn and stir-fry for 3–4 minutes. Transfer to a plate and set aside.

3 Heat the remaining oil in the wok or frying pan and stir-fry the onion for 3–4 minutes until softened and just beginning to colour. Add the tofu and chilli, stir-fry briefly and then add the noodles. Stir-fry for 4–5 minutes.

4 Stir in the beansprouts, Chinese chives and most of the ground peanuts, reserving a little for the garnish. Add the Quorn, the dark soy sauce and the reserved marinade.

5 When hot, spoon on to serving plates and garnish with the remaining ground peanuts and coriander leaves.

Tossed Noodles with Seafood

INGREDIENTS

Serves 4–6

350g/12oz thick egg noodles
60ml/4 tbsp vegetable oil
3 slices fresh root ginger, grated
2 garlic cloves, finely chopped
225g/8oz mussels or clams
225g/8oz raw prawns, peeled
225g/8oz squid, cut into rings
115g/4oz oriental fried fish cake, sliced
1 red pepper, seeded and cut into rings
50g/2oz sugar snap peas, topped
  and tailed
30ml/2 tbsp soy sauce
2.5ml/½ tsp sugar
120ml/4fl oz/½ cup stock or water
15ml/1 tbsp cornflour
5–10ml/1–2 tsp sesame oil
salt and freshly ground black pepper
2 spring onions, chopped, and 2 red
  chillies, seeded and chopped,
  to garnish

1 Cook the noodles in a large saucepan of boiling water until just tender. Drain, rinse under cold water and drain well.

2 Heat the oil in a wok or large frying pan. Fry the ginger and garlic for 30 seconds. Add the mussels or clams, prawns and squid and stir-fry for about 4–5 minutes until the seafood changes colour. Add the fish cake slices, red pepper rings and sugar snap peas and stir well.

3 In a bowl, mix the soy sauce, sugar, stock or water and cornflour. Stir into the seafood and bring to the boil. Add the noodles and cook until they are heated through.

4 Add the sesame oil to the wok or pan and season with salt and pepper to taste. Serve at once, garnished with the spring onions and red chillies.

Noodles with Spicy Meat Sauce

INGREDIENTS

Serves 4–6

30ml/2 tbsp vegetable oil
2 dried red chillies, chopped
5ml/1 tsp grated fresh root ginger
2 garlic cloves, finely chopped
15ml/1 tbsp chilli bean paste
450g/1lb minced pork or beef
450g/1lb broad flat egg noodles
15ml/1 tbsp sesame oil
2 spring onions, chopped, to garnish

For the sauce

1.25ml/¼ tsp salt
5ml/1 tsp sugar
15ml/1 tbsp soy sauce
5ml/1 tsp mushroom ketchup
15ml/1 tbsp cornflour
250ml/8fl oz/1 cup chicken stock
5ml/1 tsp shaohsing wine or
  dry sherry

1 Heat the vegetable oil in a large saucepan. Add the dried chillies, ginger and garlic. Fry until the garlic starts to colour, then gradually stir in the chilli bean paste.

2 Add the minced pork or beef, breaking it up with a spatula or wooden spoon. Cook over a high heat until the minced meat changes colour and any liquid has evaporated.

3 Mix all the sauce ingredients in a jug. Make a well in the centre of the pork mixture. Pour in the sauce mixture and stir together. Simmer for 10–15 minutes until tender.

4 Meanwhile, cook the noodles in a large saucepan of boiling water for 5–7 minutes until just tender. Drain well and toss with the sesame oil. Serve, topped with the meat sauce and garnished with the spring onions.

Main Course Spicy Prawn and Noodle Soup

This dish is served as a hot coconut broth with a separate platter of prawns, fish and noodles. Diners are invited to add their own choice of accompaniment to the broth.

INGREDIENTS

Serves 4–6

25g/1oz/¼ cup raw cashew nuts
3 shallots or 1 medium onion, sliced
5cm/2in lemon grass, shredded
2 garlic cloves, crushed
150g/5oz laksa noodles (spaghetti-sized rice noodles), soaked for 10 minutes before cooking
30ml/2 tbsp vegetable oil
1cm/½in square shrimp paste or 15ml/1 tbsp fish sauce
15ml/1 tbsp mild curry paste
400g/14oz can coconut milk
½ chicken stock cube
3 curry leaves (optional)
450g/1lb white fish fillet, such as cod, haddock or whiting
225g/8oz raw or cooked prawn tails, peeled
1 small Cos lettuce, shredded
115g/4oz beansprouts
3 spring onions, shredded
½ cucumber, sliced and shredded
prawn crackers, to serve

1 Grind the cashew nuts with the shallots or onion, lemon grass and garlic in a mortar with a pestle or in a food processor. Cook the noodles according to the instructions on the packet.

2 Heat the oil in a large preheated wok or saucepan, add the cashew nut mixture and stir-fry for 1–2 minutes, or until the nuts are just beginning to brown.

3 Add the shrimp paste or fish sauce and curry paste, followed by the coconut milk, stock cube and curry leaves, if using. Simmer for 10 minutes.

4 Cut the white fish into bite-sized pieces. Add the fish and prawns to the simmering coconut stock and cook for 3–4 minutes.

5 To serve, line a large serving platter with the shredded lettuce leaves. Arrange the beansprouts, spring onions and cucumber in neat piles, together with the cooked fish and noodles. Serve the salad with a bowl of prawn crackers and the broth in a stoneware, closed-rim pot.

COOK'S TIP

When cooking the fish and prawns, you may find it easier to put them in a large frying-basket before immersing them in the coconut stock.

Special Fried Noodles

Mee goreng is, perhaps, the best-known dish of Singapore. It is prepared from a wide range of ingredients.

INGREDIENTS

Serves 4–6

275g/10oz egg noodles
1 boneless chicken breast, skinned
115g/4oz lean pork
30ml/2 tbsp vegetable oil
175g/6oz raw or cooked prawn
    tails, peeled
4 shallots or 1 medium onion, chopped
2cm/¾in fresh root ginger, thinly sliced
2 garlic cloves, crushed
45ml/3 tbsp light soy sauce
5–10ml/1-2 tsp chilli sauce
15ml/1 tbsp rice vinegar or white
    wine vinegar
5ml/1 tsp sugar
2.5ml/½ tsp salt
115g/4oz Chinese leaves, shredded
115g/4oz spinach, shredded
3 spring onions, shredded

2 Slice the meat thinly against the grain. Heat the oil in a preheated wok and stir-fry the chicken, pork and prawns for 2–3 minutes. Add the shallots or onion, ginger and garlic and stir-fry for 2–3 minutes, until softened but not coloured.

3 Add the soy sauce, chilli sauce, vinegar, sugar and salt. Bring to a simmer. Add the Chinese leaves, spinach and spring onions, cover and cook for 3–4 minutes. Add the noodles, heat through and serve.

1 Bring a large saucepan of lightly salted water to the boil and cook the noodles according to the instructions on the packet. Drain and set aside. Place the chicken breast and pork in the freezer for 30 minutes to firm, but not freeze.

Vegetarian Fried Noodles

When making this dish for non-vegetarians, or for vegetarians who eat fish, add a piece of *blacan* (compressed shrimp paste). A small chunk about the size of a stock cube, mashed with the chilli paste, will add a deliciously rich, aromatic flavour.

INGREDIENTS

Serves 4

2 eggs
5ml/1 tsp chilli powder
5ml/1 tsp turmeric
60ml/4 tbsp vegetable oil
1 large onion, finely sliced
2 red chillies, seeded and
  finely sliced
15ml/1 tbsp soy sauce
2 large cooked potatoes, cut into
  small cubes
6 pieces fried bean curd, sliced
225g/8oz beansprouts
115g/4oz green beans, blanched
350g/12oz fresh thick egg noodles
salt and freshly ground black pepper
sliced spring onions, to garnish

1 Beat the eggs lightly, then strain them into a bowl. Heat a lightly greased omelette pan. Pour in half of the egg to cover the bottom of the pan thinly. When the egg is just set, turn the omelette over and fry the other side briefly. Slide on to a plate, blot with kitchen paper, roll up and cut into narrow strips. Make a second omelette in the same way and slice. Set the omelette strips aside for the garnish.

COOK'S TIP

Always be very careful when handling chillies. Keep your hands away from your eyes as chillies will sting them. Wash your hands thoroughly after touching chillies.

2 In a cup, mix together the chilli powder and turmeric. Form a paste by stirring in a little water.

3 Heat the oil in a wok or large frying pan. Fry the onion until soft. Reduce the heat and add the chilli paste, sliced chillies and soy sauce. Fry for 2–3 minutes.

4 Add the potatoes and fry for about 2 minutes, mixing well with the chillies. Add the bean curd, then the beansprouts, green beans and noodles.

5 Gently stir-fry until the noodles are evenly coated and heated through. Take care not to break up the potatoes or the bean curd. Season with salt and pepper. Serve hot, garnished with the reserved omelette strips and spring onion slices.

Spicy Peanut Rice Cakes

Serve these spicy, Indonesian rice cakes with a crisp green salad and a dipping sauce, such as Sambal.

INGREDIENTS

Makes 16

1 garlic clove, crushed
1cm/½in fresh root ginger, finely chopped
1.5ml/¼ tsp ground turmeric
5ml/1 tsp sugar
2.5ml/½ tsp salt
5ml/1 tsp chilli sauce
10ml/2 tsp fish sauce or soy sauce
30ml/2 tbsp chopped fresh coriander
juice of ½ lime
115g/4oz/generous ½ cup long-grain rice, cooked
75g/3oz/¾ cup raw peanuts, chopped
vegetable oil, for deep-frying

1 Pound together the garlic, ginger and turmeric in a mortar with a pestle or in a food processor. Add the sugar, salt, chilli sauce, fish or soy sauce, coriander and lime juice.

2 Add 75g/3oz of the cooked rice and pound until smooth and sticky. Stir the mixture into the remaining rice and mix well. With wet hands, shape 16 thumb-sized balls.

3 Spread the chopped peanuts out on a plate and roll the balls in them to coat evenly. Set aside.

4 Heat the oil in a preheated wok or deep frying pan. Deep-fry the rice cakes, three at a time, until crisp and golden. Remove and drain on kitchen paper. Serve immediately.

Malacca Fried Rice

There are many versions of this dish throughout the East, all of which make use of leftover rice. Ingredients vary according to what is available, but prawns are a popular addition.

INGREDIENTS

Serves 4–6

2 eggs
45ml/3 tbsp vegetable oil
4 shallots or 1 medium onion, finely
    chopped
5ml/1 tsp finely chopped fresh
    root ginger
1 garlic clove, crushed
225g/8oz raw or cooked prawn tails,
    peeled and deveined
5–10ml/1–2 tsp chilli sauce (optional)
3 spring onions, green part only,
    roughly chopped
225g/8oz frozen peas
225g/8oz thickly sliced roast pork,
    diced
45ml/3 tbsp light soy sauce
350g/12oz/1⅔ cups long-grain rice,
    cooked
salt and ground black pepper

2 Heat the remaining oil in a large preheated wok, add the shallots or onion, ginger, garlic and prawn tails and cook for 1–2 minutes, ensuring that the garlic does not burn.

3 Add the chilli sauce, spring onions, peas, pork and soy sauce. Stir to heat through, then add the cooked rice. Fry the rice over a moderate heat for 6–8 minutes. Turn into a dish and decorate with the egg strips.

1 In a bowl, beat the eggs well and season to taste with salt and pepper. Heat 15ml/1 tbsp of the oil in a large, non-stick frying pan, pour in the eggs and cook for about 30 seconds, without stirring, until set. Roll up the omelette, cut into thin strips and set aside.

Nasi Goreng

One of the most familiar and well-known Indonesian dishes. This is a marvellous way to use up leftover rice, chicken and meats such as pork. It is important that the rice is quite cold and the grains separate before adding the other ingredients, so it's best to cook the rice the day before.

INGREDIENTS

Serves 4–6

350g/12oz dry weight long-grain rice, such as basmati, cooked and allowed to become completely cold
2 eggs
30ml/2 tbsp water
105ml/7 tbsp oil
225g/8oz pork fillet or fillet of beef
115g/4oz cooked, peeled prawns
175g–225g/6–8oz cooked chicken, chopped
2–3 fresh red chillies, seeded and sliced
1cm/½ in cube *terasi*
2 garlic cloves, crushed
1 onion, sliced
30ml/2 tbsp dark soy sauce or 45–60ml/3–4 tbsp tomato ketchup
salt and freshly ground black pepper
celery leaves, Deep-fried Onions and coriander sprigs, to garnish

1 Once the rice is cooked and cooled, fork it through to separate the grains and keep it in a covered pan or dish until required.

2 Beat the eggs with seasoning and the water and make two or three omelettes in a frying pan, with a minimum of oil. Roll up each omelette and cut in strips when cold. Set aside.

3 Cut the pork or beef into neat strips and put the meat, prawns and chicken pieces in separate bowls. Shred one of the chillies and reserve it.

4 Put the *terasi*, with the remaining chilli, garlic and onion, in a food processor and grind to a fine paste. Alternatively, pound together using a pestle and mortar.

5 Fry the paste in the remaining hot oil, without browning, until it gives off a rich, spicy aroma. Add the pork or beef, tossing the meat all the time, to seal in the juices. Cook for 2 minutes, stirring constantly. Add the prawns, cook for 2 minutes and then stir in the chicken, cold rice, dark soy sauce or ketchup and seasoning to taste. Stir all the time to keep the rice light and fluffy and prevent it from sticking.

6 Turn on to a hot platter and garnish with the omelette strips, celery leaves, onions, reserved shredded chilli and the coriander sprigs.

Spicy Fried Rice Sticks with Prawns

This well-known recipe is based on the classic Thai noodle dish called *pad Thai*. Popular all over Thailand, it is enjoyed morning, noon and night.

INGREDIENTS

Serves 4

15g/¹⁄₂oz dried shrimps
15ml/1 tbsp tamarind pulp
45ml/3 tbsp Thai fish sauce *(nam pla)*
15ml/1 tbsp sugar
2 garlic cloves, chopped
2 fresh red chillies, seeded and chopped
45ml/3 tbsp groundnut oil
2 eggs, beaten
225g/8oz dried rice sticks, soaked in warm water for 30 minutes, refreshed under cold running water and drained
225g/8oz cooked, peeled king prawns
3 spring onions cut into 2.5cm/ 1in lengths
75g/3oz beansprouts
30ml/2 tbsp roughly chopped roasted unsalted peanuts
30ml/2 tbsp chopped fresh coriander
lime slices, to garnish

1 Put the dried shrimps in a small bowl and pour over enough warm water to cover. Leave to soak for 30 minutes until soft, then drain.

2 Put the tamarind pulp in a bowl with 60ml/4 tbsp hot water. Blend together, then press through a sieve to extract 30ml/2 tbsp thick tamarind water. Mix the tamarind water with the fish sauce and sugar.

3 Using a mortar and pestle, pound the garlic and chillies to form a paste. Heat a wok over a medium heat, add 15ml/1 tbsp of the oil, then add the beaten eggs and stir for 1–2 minutes until the eggs are scrambled. Remove and set aside. Wipe the wok clean.

--- COOK'S TIP ---

For a vegetarian dish, omit the dried shrimps and replace the king prawns with cubes of deep-fried tofu.

4 Reheat the wok until hot, add the remaining oil, then the chilli paste and dried shrimps and stir-fry for 1 minute. Add the rice sticks and tamarind mixture and stir-fry for 3–4 minutes.

5 Add the scrambled eggs, prawns, spring onions, beansprouts, peanuts and coriander, then stir-fry for 2 minutes until well mixed. Serve at once, garnishing each portion with lime slices.

INDEX

aubergines: aubergine in spicy
 sauce, 75
 beef and aubergine curry, 49

Balti baby chicken in tamarind
 sauce, 64
Balti chicken with lentils, 68
Balti fish fillets in spicy coconut
 sauce, 32
Balti lamb tikka, 54
Balti prawns in hot sauce, 38
basil, chilli beef with, 48
beansprouts: duck and ginger chop
 suey, 72
 spring rolls with sweet chilli dipping
 sauce, 23
 vegetarian fried noodles, 90
beef: beef and aubergine curry, 49
 beef strips with orange and ginger, 45
 chilli beef with basil, 48
 sesame steak, 46
 spicy meat-filled parcels, 22

cabbage: karahi shredded cabbage
 with cumin, 81
cauliflower braise, spiced, 78
chicken: Balti baby chicken in
 tamarind sauce, 64
 Balti chicken with lentils, 68
 green curry coconut chicken, 63
 Indonesian-style satay chicken, 66
 khara masala Balti chicken, 60
 nasi goreng, 93
 special fried noodles, 89
 spiced chicken stir-fry, 58
 spiced honey chicken wings, 20
 stir-fried chicken with pineapple, 58
 Szechuan chicken, 62
 Thai stir-fry chicken curry, 70
chillies: chilli beef with basil, 48
 chilli crabs, 42
 fried clams with chilli and yellow
 bean sauce, 18
 spring rolls with sweet chilli dipping
 sauce, 23
Chinese chives, Thai noodles
 with, 85
Chinese sweet-and-sour pork, 52
chop suey, duck and ginger, 72
clams: fried clams with chilli and
 yellow bean sauce, 18
coconut: Balti fish fillets in spicy
 coconut sauce, 32
 coconut rice, 37
 green curry coconut chicken, 63
 mixed vegetables in coconut
 milk, 82
 spiced coconut mushrooms, 76
 spiced prawns with coconut, 39
cod: boemboe Bali of fish, 31
 seafood Balti with vegetables, 34
cooking techniques, 13
courgettes: spicy courgette fritters with
 Thai salsa, 77
crab: chilli crabs, 42
 hot spicy crab claws, 21
curries: beef and aubergine curry, 49
 green curry coconut chicken, 63
 Malaysian fish curry, 36
 spicy meat-filled parcels, 22
 Thai stir-fry chicken curry, 70

deep-frying, 13
duck: duck and ginger chop suey, 72
 duck with Chinese mushrooms and
 ginger, 73

eggs: son-in-law eggs, 18
 spicy scrambled eggs, 78
equipment, 12

fish and seafood, 26–43

Balti fish fillets in spicy coconut
 sauce, 32
 braised whole fish in chilli and
 garlic, 33
 main course spicy prawn and noodle
 soup, 88
 sizzling Chinese steamed fish, 27
 Thai fish stir-fry, 30
 see also cod, salmon etc
fritters, spicy courgette, 77

galangal, 30, 39
ginger: beef strips with orange and
 ginger, 45

duck and ginger chop suey, 72
duck with Chinese mushrooms and
 ginger, 73
ginger juice, 17
oriental scallops with ginger
 relish, 40
green curry coconut chicken, 63

honey: spiced honey chicken wings, 20
hot spicy crab claws, 21

Indonesian-style satay chicken, 66
ingredients, 8–11

karahi shredded cabbage with
 cumin, 81
khara masala Balti chicken, 60

lamb: Balti lamb tikka, 54
 paper-thin lamb with spring
 onions, 57
 spiced lamb with spinach, 56
lentils, Balti chicken with, 68

mackerel: vinegar fish, 37
main course spicy prawn and noodle
 soup, 88
Malacca fried rice, 92
Malaysian fish curry, 36
meat and poultry, 44–73
monkfish: Malaysian fish curry, 36
mushrooms: duck with Chinese
 mushrooms and ginger, 73

sesame steak, 46
spiced coconut mushrooms, 76

nasi goreng, 93
noodles, 84–90
 main course spicy prawn and noodle
 soup, 88
 noodles with spicy meat sauce, 86
 special fried noodles, 89
 spring rolls with sweet chilli dipping
 sauce, 23
 Thai noodles with Chinese chives, 85
 tossed noodles with seafood, 86
 vegetarian fried noodles, 90

orange, beef strips with ginger
 and, 45
oriental scallops with ginger relish, 40

papaya: Balti lamb tikka, 54
paper-thin lamb with spring onions, 57
pastries: spicy meat-filled parcels, 22
peanuts: Indonesian-style satay
 chicken, 66
 spicy peanut rice cakes, 91
peppers: sesame steak, 46
pineapple, stir-fried chicken with, 58
pork: Chinese sweet-and-sour pork, 52
 Malacca fried rice, 92
 nasi goreng, 93
 noodles with spicy meat sauce, 86
 savoury pork ribs with snake
 beans, 50
 spicy spareribs, 24
 twice-cooked pork Szechuan-style, 53
potatoes: Thai stir-fry chicken
 curry, 70
poultry and meat, 44–73
prawns: Balti prawns in hot sauce, 38
 main course spicy prawn and noodle
 soup, 88
 Malacca fried rice, 92
 quick-fried prawns with hot
 spices, 15
 special fried noodles, 89
 spiced prawns with coconut, 39
 spicy fried rice sticks with prawns, 94
 stir-fried prawns with tamarind, 43

quick-fried prawns with hot
 spices, 15
Quorn: Thai noodles with Chinese
 chives, 85

raita, 34
relishes: ginger, 40
 sambal, 36
rice, 91–4
 coconut rice, 37
 Malacca fried rice, 92
 nasi goreng, 93
 spicy fried rice sticks with prawns, 94
 spicy peanut rice cakes, 91

salmon stir-fry, spiced, 28
salsa, Thai, 77
sambal, 36
savoury pork ribs with snake beans, 50
scallops: oriental scallops with ginger
 relish, 40
 seared scallops with wonton
 crisps, 16
seafood and fish, 26–43
 seafood Balti with vegetables, 34
 Thai fish stir-fry, 30
 tossed noodles with seafood, 86
 see also crab, prawns etc
sesame steak, 46
shrimp paste, 39
sizzling Chinese steamed fish, 27
snacks, 14–25
snake beans, savoury pork ribs
 with, 50
son-in-law eggs, 18
soup, main course spicy prawn and
 noodle, 88
spareribs: savoury pork ribs with
 snake beans, 50
 spicy spareribs, 24
special fried noodles, 89
spinach, spiced lamb with, 56
spring onions, paper-thin lamb
 with, 57
spring rolls with sweet chilli dipping
 sauce, 23
squid: deep-fried squid with spicy salt
 and pepper, 17
star anise, 28
starters, 14–25
steaming, 13
stir-frying, 13
sweetcorn: spicy scrambled eggs, 78
Szechuan chicken, 62

tamarind: Balti baby chicken in
 tamarind sauce, 64
 son-in-law eggs, 18
 stir-fried prawns with tamarind, 43
Thai fish sauce, 48
Thai fish stir-fry, 30
Thai noodles with Chinese chives, 85
Thai stir-fry chicken curry, 70
tofu stir-fry, spiced, 80
trout: sizzling Chinese steamed fish, 27
twice-cooked pork Szechuan-style, 53

vegetables, 74–82
 mixed vegetables in coconut milk, 82
 seafood Balti with, 34
 spiced tofu stir-fry, 80
vegetarian dishes, 74–82
vegetarian fried noodles, 90
vinegar fish, 37

water spinach with brown bean
 sauce, 82
wonton crisps, seared scallops with, 16

yellow bean sauce, fried clams with
 chilli and, 18
yogurt: raita, 34